ANNELEE MURRAY

THE FIRST LADY OF SPRINGBOK RUGBY

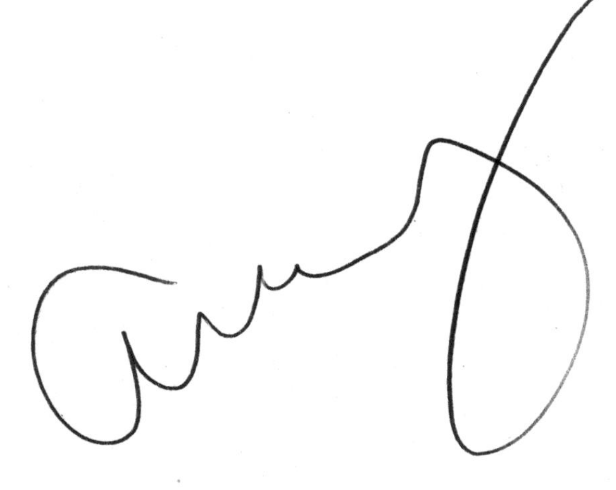

To my dad, Peter, who introduced
me to sport and always encouraged
me to follow my dreams. I miss your
love and guidance every day.

Also by Mark Keohane:

Chester
Springbok Rugby Uncovered
Champions of the World
Monty (Illustrated)
Monty
Business Day Sport Great Reads (Volume 1)
Business Day Sport Great Reads (Volume 2)
Bulletproof: The James Dalton Story
The Chosen 23

Annelee Murray: First Lady of Springbok Rugby
First published 2021

2004 03/1056/03
Highbury Media, 36 Old Mill Street, Ndabeni, 7405, Cape Town, South Africa
Second printing: October 2021
Printed by Novus Print

Editor: Zelím Nel
Copy Editor: Simon Borchardt
Proofreader: Oliver Keohane
Statistics: Kobus Smit
Design: Rashied Rahbeeni
Cover Photo: Steve Haag
Photos: Provided by Annelee Murray, unless otherwise credited

ISBN 978-0-620-94329-1.

AUTHOR'S NOTE

Why share my story?

If anything, to give every Springbok supporter some insight into the team and the players they love.

I have not experienced anything as unique as the Springbok supporters and am blessed to have enjoyed 20 years as part of team management. I've seen 248 players come through the door, worked with 21 captains, seven national coaches and many management colleagues and SA Rugby staff over the course of 244 matches.

I'd like to think what you are about to read is not so much my story but my Springbok rugby journey. It isn't about me but about the many different personalities, occasions and experiences that made my years on the road with the Boks such a remarkable memory.

I hope the book can educate and inspire supporters equally when it comes to the Springboks and the dynamics around the greatest rugby team in the world. I also hope it serves as aspiration as much as inspiration for any young woman who wants to work in sport and, in this instance, in rugby. It can be done. I am proof of that, as are several other wonderfully talented professionals who worked with me.

I hope that my journey does allow supporters to see the players differently from just men who play 80 minutes of Test rugby on a Saturday. I have tried to humanise them and articulate how I experienced working alongside them.

The highs are obvious, from the World Cup wins to the 2009 series victory against the British & Irish Lions. The lows taught me how to tackle adversity head on, and how to lean on each other when it felt like that was all we had.

I am sincerely grateful to every one of the living captains and centurions who have taken time to send a personalised message that I'm sure you'll enjoy reading.

I wanted to tell a story – filled with moments, anecdotes, observations and insights – and mostly I just wanted to celebrate Springbok rugby and the players, coaches and management who I've worked with.

I've had many a funny moment, but two that always make me laugh, if for different reasons, are when a player invited two girlfriends to a Test match and I had to spend the early part of the evening, before and during the match, managing a situation that could have been very messy for the player.

The other time was when one of the Afrikaans-speaking player's wives arrived in Wellington, New Zealand, for a Test match against the All Blacks and was stopped at customs. She was asked if she had ever taken 'narcotics' which she understood to mean '*narkose*', the Afrikaans word for anesthesia. She said yes and was duly detained by customs. It made for an interesting evening and it took the intervention of myself and the South African Embassy in Wellington to resolve the situation.

When I started with the Springboks I was as awe-struck as any fan and over time I realised the players were just as human as you and I, but it always took me by surprise when I saw how awed fans would be in their presence. It didn't matter who the fan was, they were quite star-struck to be around the guys.

One particularly memorable fan experience was when we were in the business class lounge at Gatwick Airport in London, and this youngster kept on looking our way. Eventually he approached me, very shyly, and asked if he could have a photo with Springbok winger Bryan Habana. As always, Bryan was generous with his time and the young man asked whether he would mind if the picture was posted on Instagram. Bryan had no issue with that and was later amazed to discover that the youngster was none other than Josh Devine, the drummer of the pop band, One Direction.

It has since turned into a long friendship for me as Josh loves the Springboks and has a strong connection with the country because his mother grew up in Durban.

It wasn't often I saw the Boks taking out their phones for selfie opportunities, but whenever South African golfer Ernie Els was in the room, every player wanted a photo memory of meeting Ernie. Equally, the late Nelson Mandela.

I loved my time with the Springboks and they will forever be my rugby family.

I am grateful for every opportunity I have had with the Springboks in the past 20 years and the sharing of my journey in the chapters that follow is as much a thank you to everyone as it is an introduction to my journey with the Springboks.

Annelee
Cape Town, July 2021

AUTHOR'S NOTE

It was a privilege to articulate Annelee's Springbok journey of the past 20 years. I worked with Annelee in the early part of her time with the Springboks and in the media for the rest of her journey. She has always been a loyal and beautiful friend and the absolute professional when it came to her job and the Springboks.

I don't know of anyone who cares as much about every single aspect of the Springboks and whose love is so unconditional for those who wear the green and gold of the Springboks.

She has experienced an incredible journey and her 20 years with the Springboks will be the envy of every Bok supporter.

A very good friend of mine, Craig Cloete, many years ago asked me when I was going to write Annelee Murray's book.

'Now that is a book I would buy and that is a story I would want to read,' he said.

Well, Craig, Annelee's given you an early Christmas present.

She's told the story of her journey and, for those of you who love the Springboks, it is a must-read.

Keo
Cape Town, July 2021

Contents

Contents

John Smit – Bok captain and centurion

My Springbok career started in 2000 and when I met Annelee Murray I did not fully comprehend the importance she would play in my life and the lives of the boys in green and gold for the next two decades.

Every Springbok who makes his debut is introduced to Annelee and one quickly realises that she is your lifeline in understanding where to be, at what time and in what kit. She is like the all-knowing eye and provides the guidance you need whether it is your first or your 100th Test match.

Annelee found herself surrounded by a group of highly competitive alpha males but this never deterred her and she quickly became the matriarchal woman herding 'her' boys. She was always organised, knew what was happening, and had a solution to every problem, and she most certainly had a stern voice when some of her boys needed steering back into line. All these traits, coupled with a deep caring approach for us, ensured that she quickly became an integral part of the Springbok engine. And dare anyone have an unkind word or action against one of 'her' boys – the lioness would rear its head and sort out the guilty party immediately.

It is hard to quantify the exact role and influence Annelee had on the Springboks over the almost two decades she was with the team as her role evolved from a job to becoming her family. I can only explain that no player has gotten married without Annelee being present as she became not only an important person to the player but to his wife/girlfriend too.

Annelee always tried to make the guys' lives as easy as possible and that sometimes meant creating a protective barrier around the team and absorbing pressures and stress so that the boys could focus on the job at hand on the Saturday. This sometimes meant dealing with girlfriends, wives, parents, friends, sponsors and fans. Her ability to sort things out effectively and efficiently made everyone's lives in the Bok environment so much easier.

I know that most people – including wives - preferred dealing with Annelee as she always knew what was going on.

With almost 250 Test matches under her belt, Annelee became irreplaceable in the team environment, and anyone who has been part of this environment knows the importance and value she added. I don't even think SA Rugby will fully understand how important Annelee was in the Springboks attaining their many achievements in her time with the team. While she might not have been physically present on the field, she deserved each win and carried the burden of each loss as if she were playing. I know that her time with the team has come to an end but her love for the boys in green and gold will never stop. It is in her blood.

Thinking back on my time with the Boks, I can't imagine it without Annelee there. She was always there to assist me in my role in the team and be a sounding board when I needed someone to listen to. Not only was she an incredible colleague to work with and someone I respected but she became a trusted confidant to both me and my family.

It has been such a privilege to work alongside the First Lady of Springbok rugby who gave so much of herself for almost two decades. She is the godmother to my son, and most importantly, someone I call my friend.

Chapter 1

BIG DISAPPOINTMENT, GIANT TEARS

I don't know if it was 30 or 35 minutes into the 2019 World Cup final, but this wasn't how I imagined it. I was in the Yokohama Stadium medical room with Lood de Jager. His shoulder was gone. He was physically in pain, but emotionally he was crushed. He knew his World Cup final was over.

I tried to console him. So did his mother, Juanita, and his wife, Constance.

There are strict seating and access protocols at World Cup matches but I'd managed to get to them when Lood went down 20 minutes into the final and the match director, Brendan Morris, had kindly allowed me to take them to the medical room, which ordinarily would be strictly off limits.

We were leading the final by just one Handré Pollard penalty when Lood went down and I left my seat to assist him. The score was 3-0.

It had been a brutal start to the final and England prop Kyle Sinckler had been knocked out in a contact collision three minutes after kick-off. I had cringed when he crashed to the ground in trying to make a tackle.

Look, I don't do Springbok matches well. I don't care what happens in the week, how good it has looked, how bad it appears or how confident the players and coaches are, when it comes to the Test match Saturday kick-off, I am always an emotional mess.

I know that I am the Ice Maiden from the moment the end whistle goes on a Saturday to that moment the first whistle blows on the next Saturday, but for those 80 minutes of any Test match my mind is everywhere. It has nothing to do with the team or the coaches. It is me. I am a nervous wreck.

I have a few people I text, from just before kick-off and then throughout the game. One of my favourites is Roxy Smit, the wife of John Smit. We share the same anxiety when the Springboks play, although Roxy's stress levels would have subsided significantly since Smitty retired in 2011.

My questions and statements, over 20 years and 244 Springbok matches, without fail, go like this: 'What do you think? … Really? … OK … I am not so sure … they aren't a bad team … I know how good we are but do you know who the referee is? What did you think? That was good hey … is it safe? We are going to win. Do you think we can win?' And the one that all the people I love and who I text like to mock me with when we are leading by two scores and there is one minute to go: 'It is over, hey, we are going to win, hey?' Immediately followed by: 'Are you sure?'

And equally, the text message when we aren't leading by two scores but trailing by two scores with a minute to go: 'Oh F**k'.

But right at that moment, in the medical room, nothing seemed to matter. Not the score, not the result and certainly not me.

Lood was in tears. His mother was in tears. His wife was in tears.

This was a World Cup final and in the medical room, the only thing that separated one team's player from the other was a bed.

Kyle was there and he had been there for 20, maybe 30 minutes.

He looked finished.

He just sat on the bed, staring at us and looking at the television screen in the medical room, which was showing the final.

I felt such sympathy for him.

In that moment, he wasn't the opposition and he wasn't wearing an England jersey; he was just a player whose World Cup final was over, whose dream was over and who looked dazed, disorientated and not quite aware of the situation.

I had spent the past 10 minutes with Lood, ensuring he was tended to and that his family knew he was OK. It was as if the final wasn't being played. Lood was my concern. I had to make sure he was getting the best attention, but at some point, I glanced up at the television screen and caught Kyle's eye. I smiled at him, sympathy written all over my face, and he smiled back. It was a very sweet moment and so out of sync with the occasion.

He was looking up at the television screen and watching the final. I followed his gaze to the screen and for a moment we both watched as Handré kicked a penalty.

I don't even know if Lood registered that the Springboks had scored three points and I don't recall appreciating that we had added three more points to our tally, but the television screen read 9-6 to the Springboks with 39 minutes played in the first half.

Kyle's expression hadn't changed and he asked me who was winning.

I said the Springboks were winning and, with no change to his expression, he quietly and so politely said: 'Thank you'.

It was such a powerful moment for me and I just wanted to hug him, but my attention turned to Lood, who was insistent that his Springbok jersey stayed on and that he would finish the final. His defiance was everything anyone in the team would have expected, but he was in tears.

The doctor needed to assess his shoulder and, to do it, he had to cut Lood's jersey to get it off his body. The injury was to his shoulder and he couldn't lift the shoulder to take the jersey off.

Lood initially refused because it meant destroying the jersey.

It was his World Cup final jersey, he groaned. He wasn't taking it off. He wouldn't allow it to be cut off. He told the doctor that he would have to do his examination with the jersey on.

The only comfort I could give Lood, right at that moment, was to remind him that he had two jerseys for the final, one for each half, and that the doctor had to cut the jersey off to assess the injury. I told him he still had the other jersey and that he would always have a World Cup final jersey. I tried to calm him with words like 'you will always be a World Cup final Springbok,' and that 'he had started the World Cup final'.

He was in so much pain. I felt helpless, as did his wife and mom, and collectively we all just wanted to hold him.

The final seemed so far away but, at best, it was only 50 metres away.

I looked at Kyle; he was still a blank from the concussion. I looked at Lood and he was just mad with the situation. But both had that disbelieving look that this had happened to them. My mention of 'two jerseys' seemed to resonate with Lood and he paused and reconsidered his resistance to having the jersey cut off his body. I say it like it was a calculated decision on his part, but I know it wasn't, but that's how I saw the moment. Something about that moment seemed to instinctively register with him. He knew that his World Cup final was gone, but he also knew that his World Cup final jersey wasn't gone. There was another one.

That moment must have lasted only 20 seconds but it felt like 20 minutes before Lood agreed to have his Springbok jersey cut from his body, so that the doctor could establish the extent of his shoulder injury. Listening to his moans and seeing the expression of the doctor drove home the fact that Lood's World Cup was over. All I wanted to do was cry. I know Juanita and Constance felt the same way.

Corné Krige – Bok captain

It is a massive honour for me to write a few words about Annelee.

I captained the Springboks in a very difficult period in South African rugby. There was always a lot happening off the field, and yet one person remained the same and was always a rock of support for me. Annelee always had my back and could never do enough to try and help take the pressure off me as a captain.

Despite some coaches not wanting any disruptions, Annelee believed that the players needed their families at certain times. It was the early days of wives and girlfriends being included and she jumped through many hoops for all of us to have our loved ones close when we needed them the most.

The groundwork was done for the players and captains that came after us as the team became more focused on accommodating the wives, girlfriends and children.

I will always be grateful to Annelee as she really made my life as a captain a whole lot better when we were on tour.

Chapter 2

RASSIE AND JAKE: ALL ABOUT THE RUGBY

I didn't sleep much the night before the 2019 World Cup final but it took me back to 2007 in Paris, France, which I felt was a good omen. There was so much that was familiar and similar. Jake White in 2007 and Rassie Erasmus in 2019 were carbon copies of each other in how the players believed in them, their selections and their game plan.

Having worked with both coaches, they may be very different as people and individuals but there is nothing that separates them when it comes to their primary function, which is to coach and manage the Springboks.

Both were decisive in what they did and both empowered players, but neither would put one individual before another and never would an individual be seen as bigger than the team. For both of them, the thing that mattered most was the player's performance on the field. They picked players to represent the Springboks and to win Test matches, tournaments and the World Cup. Neither of the coaches tolerated sideshows and they made sure each of us in the management team were very clear about our roles.

Jake and Rassie only needed to say it once, which they did in their very first sessions, which was that they coached rugby and they made the rugby calls. Rassie had a lovely saying, which translated from Afrikaans to English is that everyone carries their own bag. It sounds much better in Afrikaans: '*Elke een dra sy eie tassie*.' He didn't want individuals getting caught up in issues that had nothing to do with them and he didn't want individuals going out of their field of expertise and crossing into lanes in which they could only cause confusion.

Rassie asked every management member to do their job to the best of their ability and he and the coaches promised to do the same. It was a similar message to the players, in that he asked them to be the captain of their positions and not 'bullshit' themselves about their performance. It is a word Rassie used a lot and it was very effective because the players and management knew that when he used it, his tone was one of disdain.

If one thing annoyed Rassie, it was when he felt a player was not being honest with himself about his training, commitment or match-day performance and he was consistent in his messaging that the only way we would ever be successful as a champion team was if we didn't 'bullshit' ourselves. If there was honesty, there would be satisfaction and while that honesty wasn't always going to translate into a win, it meant we would be able to live with ourselves and live with each other.

The two coaches are cut from a similar cloth in that they only wanted what was best for the Springboks. Jake only ever wanted to win and he always believed the Springboks would win the 2007 World Cup in France. Rassie's belief in 2018 that the Springboks would win the World Cup in 2019 was a mirror image to what I had seen with Jake in 2004.

Both had inherited a situation in which the Springboks were at a low. When Jake took over, the Springboks had endured a very difficult 2003 and a very disappointing 2003 World Cup in losing 29-9 to the All Blacks in the quarter-finals in Melbourne, Australia. Rassie, when he took charge of the Springboks, also had to deal with the team being ranked seventh in the world and on the receiving end of some of the biggest defeats in Bok history.

Both, however, saw only the possibility of winning and were infectious with this positivity.

I had experienced such joy in Paris in 2007 when John Smit led the Springboks to victory against England. I knew the feeling of being on top of the rugby world, just like I had known that feeling of being at the bottom of the rugby pile and unsure if the Springboks could ever recover. I knew which feeling I wanted and I was convinced that Japan 2019 was going to bring the same result as that wonderful night in Paris in 2007.

I thought that, but I didn't say it out loud to anyone because I didn't want to jinx anything – rugby players and coaches, like in all sports, are often superstitious. You sit in a certain seat on the bus, the team wins a big game and that is where you sit the next time. You wear a certain tracksuit top and you get a great result and you ensure that's the tracksuit top that is worn the next time. Players would have rituals, of one boot put on before the other, of one particular underpants worn on match day, of a certain song being played and of a routine not being changed if the result the previous week had been a good one. Lose, and the superstitious among us could privately also take comfort from the fact that someone must have tampered with the routine or the winning formula.

Rassie didn't have pre-match superstitions and all I can remember is that Jake always carried a pennant on the inside of his Springbok blazer. Both were dogmatic and simple in the articulation of their message to the players: train well, prepare well, rest well and play well. Their view was that if the players did that consistently, the results would also be consistent.

It was all about rugby for both coaches. Players were picked because they were good rugby players and not because they wanted them to be good role models and ambassadors to South Africa. Both, as coaches, believed that if the individuals played well and collectively combined for a winning result, then that made them good ambassadors to the country and that made them rugby role models to any youngster who wanted to be a Springbok. No player was left in any doubt that all Jake and Rassie wanted of them was to be the best rugby players they could be, and once they were winners the rest would follow. Players would take ownership of their own image, their own on- and off-field behaviour and recognise that they had a responsibility to themselves and the jersey because they lived it and weren't merely repeating the words of the Springboks' code of conduct.

In 20 years of being with the Springboks, I've seen the good, the bad and the ugly, but the 2007 and 2019 World Cup campaigns were just so good, and I don't say that with the benefit of hindsight.

My diary reflects just how good it was, in every aspect. In France, in 2007, the Springboks were a popular team. They were based in Paris for the majority of the tournament, and the management and players culturally embraced one of the great cities of the world. The French locals loved the Springboks and often the hotel foyer in Paris would be packed with supporters wearing green and gold. None of them could speak English or Afrikaans and some of the players tried to put to use the French lessons the squad had taken before the World Cup.

The players also loved being in Paris because they could move around without being the centre of attention. It was very different to what the players would experience in New Zealand in 2011, where if they blinked someone noticed it, someone wrote about it on social media and the pressure of rugby was unrelenting.

Paris was just magnificent for the players and management, and for all of us it was not dissimilar to Japan in 2019, if very different culturally. The off-field team-related demands on the players were more with the evolvement of professionalism from 2007 to 2019, but there was such respect from the locals for every team participating in the tournament and players spoke of always feeling an atmosphere of celebration wherever they went and of goodwill from the locals.

I've been fortunate to attend the World Cups in Australia (2003), France (2007), New Zealand (2011), England (2015) and Japan (2019) and I will always remember Japan as my most enjoyable and most memorable. Every World Cup was an occasion to be cherished and every host country had a unique appeal, but the people of Japan just made 2019 something out of the ordinary. The Japanese people were incredible, and the players and management quickly fell in love with the people and the efficiency with which everything was done and the respect that was always shown towards each of us.

It was such a humbling experience to interact with the locals and I know that it will be a country that I visit often in the future because of its cultural delights and people. The players who spent time playing professionally in Japan before the World Cup, and management team members who had done recon on operational requirements leading up to the tournament, had spoken glowingly of the country, the people and their love for rugby. These players had shared their experiences with the squad when we were back in South Africa and they weren't exaggerating about how the locals would embrace the squad and also the tournament. They had warned their teammates and the management that the Japanese loved their very own Brave Blossoms and the All Blacks, but they also qualified this by saying the Japanese loved a winning team. The Japanese also resonated with people who wanted to learn about their culture, respected their culture and displayed an understanding of their culture.

The players and management, even before we got on the plane for Japan, accepted what had to be done off the field to ensure the support of the locals, but as Rassie kept on reminding the players, it was what they did on the field that would win them the ultimate respect as players, define their World Cup and potentially their careers.

Jake's message in 2007 had been similar. He told the players to enjoy the feeling of being more popular and more loved than England when in France, but he also made sure they knew that what would really make the French love them was to beat England. When the Boks won their second pool match 36-0 against England in Paris, Jake would constantly remind the players how much the French loved them for it.

'You see,' he would say. 'Now they really do love you.' He always said it with that mischievous smile of his and I think every Springbok player, coach and member of management knew how to say: 'South Africa thirty-six and England nil,' in French. I say this because every time a local would greet us, they'd start the conversation with confirmation of the score from that night at the Stade de France in St Denis.

Paris was a powerful memory for me and everywhere I looked in the build-up to the 2019 final, I had flashbacks to 2007.

In Paris, in 2007, the Eiffel Tower had been lit up in green and gold, and the squad always took that as a sign that this was to be our World Cup. In 2019 our media conference centre's roof was lit in green and gold, and it didn't go unnoticed.

Even the presidential visits were similar, in that the squad didn't know the president of the country, Mr Mbeki in 2007 and Mr Ramaphosa in 2019, would be attending the final and addressing them at the hotel before it.

The only thing missing in Japan was the physical presence of the late President Mandela, who the players simply referred to as their Madiba in 2007 and whose spirit was as strong among the Springboks in 2019.

Everything else, in 2019, was déjà vu. I kept on feeling that we, the Springboks, had been here before, but it had been in Paris in 2007, and we had triumphed.

The build-up years were even similar. In 2006, the Springboks endured a horrible losing streak, which included losing 49-0 to Australia at Suncorp Stadium in Brisbane; in 2017, the Springboks had lost 57-0 to the All Blacks in Albany, New Zealand. It was chastening to be in the change room on both those occasions and to see the hurt, shame and embarrassment of the players. What gave me hope was that the same players of 2006 had a year later brought such cheer to the change room because of incredible wins and in 2018 many of those players who had lost 57-0 against the All Blacks were inspirational in coming from 24-3 down against England at Emirates Airline Park (Ellis Park) to win 41-38. The Springboks in 2007 had shown it was possible to rise from the dead and the class of 2019, a year earlier, had also resurrected the Springboks.

If it could be done in 2018, against England in Johannesburg and Bloemfontein, then it could be done in 2019 in the World Cup final.

I kept on looking for the signs and I kept on finding them.

The 2007 Springboks beat England in Bloemfontein and at Loftus in Pretoria before beating them twice in Paris at the World Cup.

England were the opposition in the 2007 final and once again it was England facing us in the final in 2019, although back in France in 2007, England's head coach Eddie Jones was sitting at our management table as Jake's specialist coaching and technical consultant.

Eddie is a gem and one of the great characters in world rugby. He is charming, whether he is in your team or in the opposition and his sense of humour is as dry as it can be dramatic. He is a treat to listen to but I have only known him to be all about rugby. He just loves the game and he loves talking rugby. He loves South Africa and he would always remark on the passion for the game in South Africa and the adulation there is for the Springboks.

I have always enjoyed Eddie as a person and I have experienced how much the South African players enjoy and respect him. I do believe that no matter what Eddie does or who he coaches, there will always be a bit of green and gold in him after his contribution to the 2007 World Cup win in France. Eddie had a unique World Cup record of winning the trophy with the Springboks and also beating the Springboks in 2015 when coaching Japan. He was either going to add to that record by winning a final against the Springboks or losing one. I prayed for the latter, but I knew that, whatever the result, I would be experiencing a gracious and embracing Eddie after the World Cup final. He is just that type of person and I wasn't wrong to assume that of him and that his sense of occasion would always allow for an appropriate expression of his humour, which was understated and always delivered with such charm.

The week leading into the final in Yokohama, Japan, was one of controlled chaos for me in my capacity as PR manager but one of absolute calm among the coaches and the players.

It was so like 2007 in Paris and one of my fondest memories of the final week in Paris was having a coffee with the delightful Bakkies Botha. I asked Bakkies how he was feeling and he looked at me, without his expression changing, sighed and said: '*Ag*, Annelee, I just want to play the game, fetch William and get on the plane home.'

The Wallabies were famous for referring to the Webb Ellis Cup (the World Cup trophy) as 'Bill', but for Bakkies it was simply William.

I remember leaving our coffee catch-up and giggling to myself at the way Bakkies said it – the 'fetching of William' – and every time I played back that response I would smile and then laugh out loud. It was so typical of Bakkies, his christened name being John Philip, to be so dry in his delivery of something, yet so powerful in what he was meaning.

He just knew the Boks would win, but that they would have to play well to win, and his confidence was so reassuring, it convinced me that we would win. OK, that was until kick-off, because as I have said previously, when it comes to those 80 minutes of the match, I would never believe we were winning until I heard the final whistle and the scoreboard said so.

The players in the week leading into the 2019 final were just so relaxed and the one major difference was that they didn't have the off-field distractions of being based in the city centre of Paris in 2007. The Bok team hotel was a good hour to an hour-and-a-half's drive outside of the main city centre in 2019 — this was by choice and part of the management's pre-tournament planning.

The players were comfortable to have the space and the quality of an environment that helped them to focus and also allowed them to be with their partners, wives and families.

One of the biggest evolutions in the Springboks' squad culture throughout my 20 years was the integration of the family into the squad environment when it came to Test matches at home and especially during World Cups, and the 2019 experience was the most inclusive it had ever been since the first of my 244 Springbok matches dating back to 2001.

Rassie is very big on family involvement and inclusivity and he met with me for input based on my experience of catering and accommodating family over my many campaigns. It may be a cliché but it is true, that a player who is happy at home is a player who is happy in camp. We always tried to replicate as much of a home environment as possible and create that environment within the team, especially when it came to the wives, partners and children.

What set the Springboks apart from other teams at the 2019 World Cup was this family unit, in which the players enjoyed having their families with them on tour. Though there were areas – like the team rooms – which were off-limits, sharing their hotel room with their family calmed the players because their off-time was spent with the most precious people in their lives. They didn't feel like they were on tour and, having the partners, wives and children close meant they could find a release from the pressures of the tournament and the demanding training schedules. Once they left the field, they went back to their hotel rooms and it was like going back to their home living rooms. When they walked through the door, they saw the faces they loved the most. I can't emphasise enough how powerful that was in the emotional well-being of every player and it should be a lesson to every Springbok coach in the future.

I always knew that the World Cup final week would be my biggest one of the tournament, but even though I had experienced four World Cups I couldn't have predicted the intensity of this fifth one in Japan. It was an intensity that came from the South African public in their support and love for the team.

So much has changed since my first Test and technology is the most obvious. In the early years our team room was always filled with messages of support pasted to the walls. Those were back in the days of fax machines, but in 2019 it was all technologically driven and team associate sponsor FNB were primary to ensuring the presence and managing of electronic platforms in which the public could send messages, pictures and videos. The players, coaches and management, without exception, spent time having a look at what the people were posting and this helped them live the mood back in South Africa. It was amazing to get a sense of what people were feeling and how important the team's success was to the people back home. We really are unique as South Africans when it comes to our relationship with the Springboks, and I say this as a South African who loves the team and as someone who was part of the Springboks for two decades. There is a bond between player and supporter that is so powerful and so aligned to a national loyalty and patriotism.

I can tell you the players and coaches feel it and they are never just playing for the satisfaction of a victory. It doesn't matter who played, captained or coached the Springboks in my time, the overriding constant was their belief that they were doing this for the people of South Africa and that somehow a Springbok victory was always more than a sporting result. If the people of South Africa love the Springboks, all I can tell the people of South Africa is those players love them and never take their support for granted.

It's a crazy situation because the power of the Springbok is on another level for South Africans. One example that springs to mind is when we arrived back from a successful overseas tour, and Breyton Paulse and I had to be rescued from the public adulation for the Boks as we were isolated in a mass of celebrating supporters. I've witnessed the country's most celebrated individuals, in business, arts and politics, be seduced when they step into the Springbok environment.

It doesn't seem to matter who they are or what they have achieved in their profession or chosen career path, they are awed when they interact with the Springboks, which doesn't mean the players aren't as awed in who they are meeting.

I remember the players being rather awestruck in meeting South African entrepreneur Mark Shuttleworth in London in 2002, as he was invited to address the team and present the jerseys to the players on the eve of the Test match against England. He delivered such an emotive speech to them and told them that they were unique in wearing the jersey and that it was an experience that couldn't be bought and had to be earned.

I only wish the squad had been more experienced because we had a very young team on tour and the selectors had left 20 senior players at home to rest or rehabilitate for the pending 2003 World Cup year, and we got thrashed by England the next day. This was one occasion when the hype of the pre-match jersey ceremony and the speech of the guest was far greater than the performance the next day.

There was no such fear in Japan in the week of the World Cup final that the on-field performance would in any way be inferior, but that wasn't because the pre-match rituals would be anything less than spectacular.

To the contrary, we'd only got word 48 hours before the final that President Ramaphosa would be flying to Japan to attend the final and would only get to Japan on the morning of the final, which meant that my week was only about to get more frantic, even if it was the best kind of frantic.

André Vos – Bok captain

Twenty years ago it certainly wasn't commonplace for women to be closely associated with rugby teams. That all changed when Annelee joined the Springbok setup, much to the benefit of the team and South African rugby.

Annelee definitely brought a softer touch to what can sometimes be a tough and demanding environment.

Guys don't always do so well with feelings and emotions. Outside her day-job responsibilities, Annelee added a new dimension to the support provided by the Springbok management team. In doing so, she filled a big gap which most of us didn't even realise needed filling.

Living away from home for up to seven months of the year can be difficult, especially for the guys in long-term relationships. Annelee was extremely supportive of the wives and girlfriends. She made a point of fighting for an inclusive approach which made the ladies feel wanted and welcomed within the team setup.

Annelee celebrated with us in victory, but she was also a consoling presence when the results didn't go our way, and a voice of reason when one was sorely needed.

Annelee became a good friend to many of the guys. She was a fellow coffee-appreciator and a much-needed fashion consultant when we toured places like Italy and other trendy destinations. And a reminder of perspective and balance, when these were sometimes lost during a long international season.

SA Rugby and the players have certainly come to realise how much we owe to this unassuming but very special lady.

Thank you Annelee for sharing so freely, and for giving your all.

We appreciate and value you.

Chapter 3

PREPARING FOR THE BIGGEST MATCH OF THEM ALL

Rassie Erasmus insisted that he didn't want the players to know President Ramaphosa would be meeting them until he was actually at the hotel. He didn't want anything to distract the players, so the president's visit had to be an added bonus to the match-day schedule.

I don't know what initially was more nerve-racking, hiding the arrival of the president, or Eben Etzebeth's secret plan to get Jesse Kriel and Trevor Nyakane back to Japan for the final.

Eben came to see me once we had beaten Wales in our semi-final and said we had to find a way to bring back Jesse and Trevor, both of whom had been forced out of the tournament with injuries, and that no one in the team could know we were planning this. He wanted the return of Jesse and Trevor to be a surprise and another boost for the team on match day. The players were a very close group and there was obvious disappointment when Jesse and Trevor had to return to South Africa. Eben knew what impact it would have on the squad to see them walk through the door on the Saturday morning and he took it upon himself to make it happen.

I knew that I had to make a plan so I suggested we call Gavin Varejes, who is among the most ardent supporters of the Springboks. Gavin, a prominent business personality in South Africa, is also the president of the South African Rugby Legends Association. He has done so much for the players ever since I've known him and he has never thought twice about giving to the cause of the players and the Springboks. Gavin has always been particularly generous with his time and very charitable in funding when it comes to anything to do with the Springboks, particularly in promoting the Legends and ensuring that those players who served South African rugby are not forgotten. Gavin isn't someone who publicly promotes all that he does, but it has always been huge.

Eben called Gavin, explained the situation and asked if there was any way he could financially assist in getting Jesse and Trevor on a plane. Gavin didn't hesitate in agreeing and 'all' that remained was for me to liaise with his PA Tanya Harvey and the Japanese Embassy for visas. I have deliberately emphasised the 'all' because it would take some manoeuvring to sort out the visas, and it wasn't quite as simple as getting the players on a flight to Japan from South Africa a few days before the World Cup final.

I also had to make a plan to ensure we could find a room at the hotel for Jesse and Trevor. I fear that somewhere in the world there is a disgruntled couple who may have missed out on a hotel room that weekend.

Thankfully, the Japanese Embassy was as helpful as they had been from the moment that I started dealing with them. Nothing seemed to be too much effort and, as I have mentioned several times, the Springboks were very popular in Japan and inside the walls of the embassy.

It would be a scramble for visas and Tanya worked her magic to ensure Jesse and Trevor got onto a plane. Once again, I felt like I was back in Paris in 2007, only then I was arranging to get Pierre Spies and Jean de Villiers to the City of Love for the final. Pierre had been selected for the 2007 World Cup squad but forced to withdraw because of injury before the team departed, and Jean had torn a bicep muscle in the Boks' opening game of the World Cup against Samoa.

In 2007, as was the case in 2019, the charity of Gavin was responsible for reuniting both players with the squad as he funded their flights from South Africa to France.

Fast forward to the World Cup final week in 2019 and, Trevor and Jesse aside, most of my week was spent ensuring the Springbok squad members' ticket requests for the final were sorted and that all the wives, partners, parents and families were good to go.

Then there were the VIP and sponsor ticket requests, followed by more ticket requests and more ticket requests. I'd learned over the years to take a breath and calm myself, but in those 48-72 hours before a Test it is overwhelming when everything seems to come at you at once.

In a World Cup final week, particularly, it is madness because nothing can be actioned until you have won the semi-final and qualified for the final. Win, and your week takes a very different turn; lose, and you're playing the dreaded 'third-place playoff'. And if you lose in the quarter-finals, you have to be out of the country within 24 hours of the result.

I'd experienced that in New Zealand in 2011 when we lost to Australia in our quarter-final and it was emotionally and physically draining, a logistical nightmare and just awful, so preparing for all the sideshows of a final was bliss in comparison.

Once again, I found myself thinking back to Paris in 2007, only this time I didn't have John Smit's wife, Roxy, there as support to get through all the administration and process every request. Roxy was a dream whenever she was on tour. She'd just roll up her sleeves and get on with it.

In Japan, there was no Roxy and I settled into World Rugby's tournament offices where I spent six hours over a two-day period doing the tickets, the allocations and the organisation for the final. I was in possession of millions of rands worth of tickets for VIPs, sponsors and dignitaries and the safest place to work was at World Rugby's offices, but even when there I'd have moments when I thought 'oh my goodness, I can't lose these tickets' and, 'these have cost millions'. The long taxi ride back to Tokyo Bay was also nerve-racking with this precious cargo.

There was not only planning around the match in the week but also the post-match tasks. If the Springboks won there were certain protocols that had to be followed and certain responsibilities. If they lost, the picture changed radically, but there were still things the team had to do. We had to plan for both eventualities, as a management. For example, the entire winning team was expected to attend the World Rugby Awards, held the night after the final, but the losing team only sent the players who had been nominated for awards and their coach.

In a worst-case scenario result, the players would only be privy to everything once that result became a reality, but the management had to operate in a parallel planning week as a World Cup winner and loser.

Whatever the result, the show goes on. It is something I learned after my first home Test, which ended in a shock defeat against France at Ellis Park in 2001. Win or lose, nothing changes in the way the team management is expected to complete whatever responsibility is in one's portfolio.

All week I was planning for the win, but also being part of the management team's planning for defeat, which didn't always make it pleasant because emotionally it becomes a roller-coaster ride. You have to plan for the possibility of coming second but your heart isn't in it, which doesn't mean there can be any less application in effort.

What makes it more palatable is seeing just how much support there is for the team and the confidence from within the travelling support, the people back in South Africa and obviously the players and coaches. But it was a week in which I just operated on adrenaline and I know it was the same for every one of the management team.

What made it so much more bearable in the World Cup final week is that the squad was based in Tokyo Bay, a little more than an hour's drive from the Yokohama venue of the final, which meant there was always relative calm at the team hotel. It was very different to Paris in 2007 when the Boks were based in the city centre for the semi-final and final weeks.

Having the families ever-present also added to the calmness, especially in the 48 hours before the final and for the players they were as close to a home environment as possible. The extended families who flew in a couple of days before the final were also welcome visitors at the team hotel and absolutely nothing about the World Cup final week changed, in terms of preparation when compared to any other week of the tournament.

It was a short week because we'd played the semi-final on Sunday and would face England in the final six days later, which meant one less training day. But the established patterns and routines were working and the players were comfortable in a schedule where they knew what was expected of them and when. There was no grey area in the schedule about when it was match preparation time and when they could switch off to be with their families. It had been that way since we arrived in Japan, which was a fortnight before the World Cup.

It was a masterstroke from Rassie to play Japan in Japan before the World Cup. The Springboks had only ever played Japan once, a match which is infamous among South Africans and famous among the Japanese, as Japan won in the last movement of the match in Brighton, England, at the 2015 World Cup. Rassie didn't want the Boks having to play Japan at the World Cup with the memory of 2015 suffocating them. He wanted the 2019 team to create a new Japan memory, which was beating them in Japan.

Everything we did in the warm-up match and weeks before the World Cup replicated what we would do during the World Cup, and the belief was that the team in the World Cup would repeat the 41-7 result we achieved against Japan. The players got accustomed to the humidity, the pace at which Japan played the game and also the fanaticism of the Japanese supporters.

There was an expectation back in South Africa that the Springboks should easily beat Japan, but you had to be in the country to get an appreciation of just how frenzied the support was for the hosts. You also had to experience the humidity to fully grasp how tough it was on our players, with most of the squad not having been exposed to that level of humidity.

I said it earlier that this was a World Cup like no other and that was down to the manner in which the locals embraced and supported every team playing in the tournament. There was the natural support for Japan but then supporters adopted a second team and treated that team with the same reverence as they did Japan. When it came to the locals who had taken the Springboks in as their own, the experience for all of us was remarkable. When we visited schools to do coaching clinics or had signing sessions or were part of any formal engagement, the local contingent – which numbered in the thousands – sang our national anthem to perfection, were dressed in green and gold, hoisted our South African flag with pride and gave each open training session a home feeling. We had anything from 5 000 to 10 000 people at those training sessions and it was very foreign to our players who were used to playing in front of the biggest crowds but not always used to training in front of crowd that numbered 10 000.

The players were idolised and the locals knew each player's name and position when wanting autographs, and they had their favourites, with Faf de Klerk particularly prominent when it came to the signing sessions.

I talk about the magnitude of the final but every week at the World Cup felt big and after we lost to the All Blacks in our first match, every week felt like a final because if we lost again, we'd be out of the tournament. The New Zealand game was massive and there was such belief that we would win, given we'd beaten the All Blacks in Wellington in 2018, led 30-13 in Pretoria in 2018 before losing 32-30, and drawn 16-16 in Wellington in 2019.

There was such respect between the players from the All Blacks and Springboks. It has always been like that and the match at the World Cup typified every bit of respect between the two teams. We lost by 10 points in Yokohama but it could easily have been a case of us winning by 10 points. I am not going to go into the intricacies of the rugby because that's not my field of expertise, but here I am putting my supporter's cap on and this supporter's cap felt we were going to win. When we didn't, I was pretty shattered even though the management squad member in me had to put on a brave face and get on with it.

The All Blacks game, colossal as a contest, was not as big as the quarter-final against Japan, who had the support of the rest of the rugby world when they played us. Please don't misinterpret my words to mean we believed the world was against us because we were South African. It was more that the world was against us because we were playing Japan. It didn't matter who Japan played in the quarter-final, everyone in world rugby wanted them to succeed. They were the fairy-tale story of the tournament and they had already beaten Ireland and Scotland in the pool stage. It wasn't madness for them to believe they could beat us because they had in 2015. It also wasn't an improbability, which is what Rassie hammered home to the players all week. He made sure each player knew that to win we'd have to play well. This wasn't a matter of pitching up and winning on reputation.

The World Cup final week has its own intensity, simply because it is a final, but that quarter-final week, preparing to play the hosts Japan, had a mental intensity of a very different kind to the final.

We were up against a nation in that week, as well as the goodwill of the rest of the rugby world. It wasn't personal, but in the context of the tournament it was predictable in how everyone rallied around Japan, which made the response of Rassie, his coaches and the players that much more remarkable.

Rassie's leadership style meant he didn't dwell on the defeat against the All Blacks because he told the players and management that we still had a second chance in the tournament and a chance at creating history at the World Cup. No team had ever lost a pool match and won the World Cup. He challenged the players to be the first to do so after we lost to the All Blacks, and he was one of a few I heard predict that Japan would qualify for the quarter-finals and that they were good enough to beat Ireland during the pool stage.

I had been in Brighton in 2015 when Japan had not been given the necessary credit as an opponent. Fourie du Preez had warned Heyneke Meyer about Eddie Jones and the Japan threat. Fourie had spent a few seasons playing in Japan at Suntory, who were coached by Eddie. Fourie and Eddie were very close and the two have the utmost respect for each other. Fourie won't hesitate to tell you how highly he rates Eddie, and Eddie has often been quoted on the virtues of Fourie as being one of the best rugby players he has ever coached. Fourie was filthy and very upset after the Japan defeat because he felt his words of caution had not been taken seriously, but those who played in 2015 and were around in 2019 didn't need a reminder of the threat of Japan.

Rassie, in management meetings, spoke of Japan as he would the All Blacks, England and Wales. He acknowledged what they had achieved as a unit and the qualities of Jamie Joseph and Tony Brown as the Japan coaches. Jamie and Tony had played for the All Blacks and Rassie had played against Tony at Super Rugby and Test levels. There was something spectacular about how these former All Blacks had managed to pick 16 naturalised foreign players and integrate them so easily into Japan's national set-up. There was an acceptance among the Japanese supporters that these players represented Japan and they were treated with the respect of those players born in Japan. Among these naturalised Japanese were a few South African-born players, which added another edge to the match.

We were very conscious as a squad of how much momentum Japan had in the week of our quarter-final against them and our players' attitudes attested to this knowledge. There was no let-up and they were as switched on for the rugby as they were for the weeks that would follow against Wales in the semi-final and England in the final.

For those not versed in the structure that is consistent with the Springboks in a Test match week, indulge me as I set it out for you because it will help you understand the day-to-day workings of the Springboks at the World Cup. There is nothing sexy about it and nothing revolutionary. It is all about structure, routine, repetition and the discipline to do it all over again the next day, with enthusiasm and with conviction.

As an example, I've used Tuesday, 29 October 2019.

SPRINGBOK FINALS TRAINING WEEK PROGRAMME

29 October 2019 to 1 November 2019

Tokyo

TUESDAY

29 October 2019

07:00 – 08:25	Breakfast
07:00 – 08:25	Coaches Meeting
09:40 – 10:10	Game Drivers' Meeting
10:15 – 11:15	Team Meeting
11:15– 12:00	Split Review
	Forwards
	Backs
2:00 – 13:00	Lunch
30 – 13:15	Media Conference
20– 13:40	Strapping
5 – 14:45	Team Preview
– 15:15	Walk-Through
	Bus depart to Training Venue
– 17:00	Field Session
17:35	Gymnasium
	Bus depart to Hilton Hotel
	Swimming
	Goal Review
	Dinner
	Collection of laundry

WEDNESDAY

30 October 2019

	Breakfast
	Coaches Meeting (Players are welcome)
	Game Drivers' Meeting
	Team Meeting
	Split Meetings
	Forwards Line-Out Detail
	Backs Passing Detail
	Lunch
	Strapping
	Media Conference
	...nd Walk Through
	session – ...

Group Massage

THURSDAY

31 October 2019

07:00 – 09:00	Breakfast
08:30 – 11:30	Group Massage
12:00 – 13:00	Media Conference
19:00	Collection of laundry

Pay-Out for Lunch and Dinner

FRIDAY

1 November 2019

07:00 – 09:00	Breakfast
07:00 – 08:45	Coaches Meeting (Players welcome)
08:55 – 09:25	Strapping
09:30 – 10:10	Jersey Presentation
10:15 – 10:20	Team Photo
10: 35 – 11:15	Strapping
11:30	Bus depart to International Stadium Yokohama
12:30 – 13:00	Team Meeting
13:00 – 14:00	Captains' Run
14:00 – 14:30	Kickers
14:00 – 14:30	Eve of Match Media Conference
14:30	Bus depart to Hotel
15:30 – 16:30	Lunch and Sleep
19:00 – 20:00	Dinner
19:00	Collection of laundry

SATURDAY

2 November 2019

08:00 – 09:30	Breakfast
11:00 – 11:30	Forwards Detail Session
	Backs: Skills Detail
11:30 – 12:00	Lunch
13:30:00	Logistics depart to Yokohama International Stadium

14:30 – 15:30	Pre-match meal	
13:40 – 15:10	Strapping	
14:00 – 14:30	Pre-Match Meal	
15:15 – 15:25	Team Talk	
15:30	Bus depart to Yokohama International Stadium	
16:30	Bus arrives at Yokohama International Stadium	
16:35	Pre-Match Interview with the Head Coach	
16:35 – 17:05	Additional Strapping	
16:52 - 16:57	Equipment check and Referee instructions to captain, front rows and scrumhalf	
17:00	Coin Toss	
17:13 – 17:45	Pre-match Warm-Up Drills	
17:13	Kickers Out	
17:18	Hookers Out	
17:21	Props Out	
17:24	Rest of the Team Out	
17:45	South Africa return to Change Rooms	
17:54	South Africa leaves Change Rooms and Line-Up in the Tunnel	
17:55	South Africa and walk to the Field of Play	
	National Anthems	
18:02 – 18:45	**South Africa vs (first half)**	
18:45 – 19:00	Half Time (15 minutes)	
18:57	South Africa leaves the Change Rooms and run on to the Field of Play	
19:00 – 19:45	**South Africa vs (second half)**	
19:45	On-field interviews	
	+2:10	Losing Captain
	+3:30	Winning Captain
	+5:30	Losing Coach
	+6:45	Winning Coach
	+7:55	Man of the Match
	Post-Match Huddle	
19:55	Recovery	
20:00 – 20:45	Post-Match Media Conference	
20:15 -20:45	+30	Losing Team
	+45	Winning Team
	Mixed Zone	
20:45 – 21:30	Bus depart to Hotel	
21:30	Team Meeting on Arrival at Hotel	
22:30 – 22:45		

Whether it was week one of the tournament or the final week, the schedule remained the schedule, and the players were confident and comfortable with the familiarity of the routine. They knew when they were required at the office and they knew when they had off-time, and at the World Cup in 2019, off-time meant time with family.

This really helped the players to switch off, especially those with young children. The dynamic changes so much when the players are interacting with their kids and know they are waiting back at the hotel room. While there was a general understanding of which zones were off-limits, like the team room, the players would balance their time between the team room, the family area and the sanctuary of their hotel room out of choice.

There was also a lot of engagement and mingling among the wives, partners and children, and as clichéd as it sounds, the 2019 group was one big happy family, in which all that the players had to focus on was playing the game of rugby. Each one of us in the management would look after their every need, be it medical, media interviews preparation, sponsor engagements, signing sessions or travel and accommodation. And when it came to family time, the partners and wives were there to be the ideal travelling companions and give them the sense and comfort of being at home.

Just having the little ones around for the players also meant there was never the kind of unrelenting tension and pressure that I had experienced at other World Cup tournaments where the pressure levels each week were heavily dependent on the most recent result.

In 2019, it was so different because of how Rassie led the response after the loss to the All Blacks. He didn't let the result affect his mentality and the defeat didn't change anything in his preparation or in the pre-determined schedules and structures. The management team and players had prepared well and we felt our formula would bring success. Win or lose, we knew what was expected of management the next day, and fortunately for us in 2019 the wins were more than the losses.

The All Blacks and Japan matches had an intensity that was big, but different to the final and my overriding sense of both build-ups was one of anticipation among the players and coaches. There was a confidence in victory that was tangible but it never bordered on an arrogance or a deluded sense of reality. Everything would have to go to plan to beat the All Blacks, and to beat Japan, our players would have to find a mental resolve to combat the collective energy of a nation.

I never doubted it was possible, but I must confess to being so nervous for the semi-final against Wales.

When I first joined the Springboks, at the turn of the century, whenever we played New Zealand or England there was something greater about the mental state of the players than for any other opponents, and in my early years it was almost accepted within the squad that a match against Wales meant a win.

While I remember some close games I never thought we would or could lose, but in Warren Gatland's era with Wales it was very different. Wales beat us and they beat us regularly. The 2015 World Cup quarter-final at Twickenham was in the balance with five minutes to play before Duane Vermeulen and Fourie du Preez combined for a brilliant try. Four years later, there was a sense that it was inevitably going to be as close in the semi-final against Wales.

Rassie was very vocal about the toughness of the Welsh and how our players had to be even tougher, and that what the Welsh lacked in finesse they made up for in their hearts. He saw a lot of similarities in the psyche of the Welsh and South African players. They had soul as a team and they had a very good coach, and I am merely repeating the words of Rassie in the semi-final week.

We won the semi-final with Damian de Allende scoring a brilliant try and Handré Pollard kicking the match-winning penalty, but unlike the quarter-final win where there had been a sense of euphoria, here it just felt like relief in the change room.

Our players knew they had been in a battle and there was acknowledgement of the quality and fight of the Welsh, whose character and tenacity spoke to all those characteristics we hold dear in the Springboks.

Wales had beaten us twice in 2018 and if there was one week where there was an anxiousness amid the excitement, I'd say it was the week of the semi-final. There was never any self-doubt, but it was definitely in the back of everyone's mind that this was a team that had beaten us in 2018 and had enjoyed a few more wins recently.

I didn't get that feeling of anxiousness from the players or coaches in the build-up to the final. Judging by what the coaches and players had to say I think they were all surprised at England's one-sided semi-final win against the All Blacks, but they weren't surprised that England won. There was very much a feeling in the camp before the game that either England or the All

Blacks could win, but everyone thought it would be a lot closer, and it was a very upbeat Eddie Jones and John Mitchell who came to our semi-final on the Sunday. They sat in the stands, close to our non-playing squad and I said hello to them. They seemed to believe they'd be seeing us in the final and gave me a wink after the final whistle as if to confirm what they had said to me before kick-off.

I am pleased to put on record that they were right to have such confidence in the Springboks.

John, a former All Blacks coach, had also coached the Lions and Bulls in South Africa and spent quite a few years involved in South African rugby. He has a love for South Africa, as a country, and for the South African rugby players, and everyone knows the soft spot Eddie has for the Springboks and the enjoyment he gets from being in rugby-mad South Africa.

I have always enjoyed Eddie and John as rugby people and they have always been consistent in their behaviour, win or lose.

Watching the England media conferences in the week of the final, Eddie and John came across as very confident, but the English players at times appeared more arrogant than confident, and this wasn't lost on us.

Rassie was a study of clarity in the World Cup final week. I don't know if inside he was feeling different, but his projection all week was that of a contented coach, who knew he and his team had done their work and that the players were mentally prepared for the biggest game of their careers.

It took me back to 2004 when Jake invited England's 2003 World Cup-winning coach Clive Woodward to speak to the Bok management about England's campaign and the journey to their success in Australia. I found Clive's talk inspiring and was intrigued by how much he spoke about the small gains that give champion teams the small margins in the build-up to matches and in the matches. Clive instilled a premium on the role of each management portfolio and how each member of the management had to be the world leader in their field of expertise, or at least believe they were the equal of anyone else.

Clive spoke of how the England management team in 2003 constantly challenged themselves and each other to be the best and find something in their portfolio that would translate into an advantage for the player and the team.

I never forgot the thread of his message that I, as part of the management, could be influential in giving a player an edge, and that the team manager, media liaison, logistics manager, physio, team doctor and baggage master all contributed to a team's success.

Our 2003 World Cup campaign in Australia had not been good and our preparation had not been ideal. Back then I felt like we all were playing catch-up and always one step behind, whereas in 2019, in the hours leading into the final, I felt so content.

I knew that within my portfolio and beyond it I had done whatever I could to ensure no player had a distraction or concern about anything relevant to his wife, partner, child or family. All the player had to worry about was his performance on the field. I knew each player's individual request had been dealt with and that the players' families were in good spirits, the match tickets were in the hands of whoever they needed to be, the sponsor commitments had been met with enthusiasm and excellence, and that this had transferred to anything the media liaison required from the players.

When I looked at the work ethic of the rest of the management team, I knew I was working with colleagues who set the standard and were among the world's best, if not the best in their profession.

In 2004 I had heard what Clive was saying when he spoke to us, and in Japan on the morning of the World Cup final in 2019, I felt I was living what he said, about the contentment in knowing there was nothing more I had to do and that it was that type of contentment that the squad would take into the biggest match of them all, a World Cup final.

On this Saturday morning, less than 12 hours before the World Cup final kick-off, I felt abnormally calm and ready to welcome the president of South Africa, Mr Cyril Ramaphosa, and, along with our team manager Charles Wessels, guide him to the room where the players were meeting, unaware of who would be coming through the doors.

Bob Skinstad – Bok captain

Annelee, a lifelong friend made overnight!

I remember meeting Annelee for the first time on Table Mountain. It was during a promotional function and little did I know at the time what a long road we would travel together.

We had some amazing times, and some difficult ones (losing is not easy for management either!), but Annelee was always the rock we could rely on to help smooth the waters and calmly navigate how we were going to forge ahead.

I recall the little printer in her room working overtime and the most amazing attention to detail which made it easy for us to be in the Springboks' all-focus mode but always feel like you were with your family.

She made a real point of helping me to host and spend time with Nelson Mandela, and made sure my wife and I were front and centre of that engagement. I was, and am, incredibly grateful!

Annelee made a lot of the special times of our lives even better and I will never forget that.

Chapter 4

PRESIDENT RIGHT ON TIME, ENGLAND LATE

Trevor Nyakane and Jesse Kriel had arrived at the hotel a few minutes before President Ramaphosa, and I had to ensure none among the squad saw them before they made their way into the team room, where the players were gathering for their scheduled 11am meeting.

Siya Kolisi was the only player put on standby for the president's arrival, as he would officially welcome him and then we'd all make our way to join the rest of the squad. There were the usual protocols whenever a head of state was nearby and the security always arrives ahead of the president and does all the usual sweeps of the place.

The players were shocked to see the president walk in, and he greeted each of them and had a chat. Nothing could ever beat the presence of the late President Mandela, but President Ramaphosa's entrance was spectacular in its own right because he had such an amazing energy about him and the players could see that from the moment he walked into the team room.

President Ramaphosa took the time to greet every single member of the squad with a handshake and he asked every one of us a question about the tournament and how we were feeling. I felt special and privileged, and I know every squad member felt the same way. President Ramaphosa treated each of us the same, which is the way we had always treated each other, but it was telling that he didn't differentiate between the player who had scored the most tries and any of the management members. If you were in that room, you had played a part in getting the Springboks to the final, and President Ramaphosa didn't mix his words when he told us that the final was more than a rugby match for the country and that it was an occasion in which we had to triumph.

'This is for the country,' he said. 'We need it. South Africa needs it.' His message was one about the mood in South Africa, the positivity around the squad, the unanimous and united support for the squad and the symbolism of what the squad represented to all South Africans. The guys were playing for themselves and each other, but if they had any doubts, they now knew they were also playing to meet the expectation of 60 million South Africans.

President Ramaphosa spoke with such sincerity about the power of sport and the Springboks in bringing together a nation, and the impact of those who had gone before, but he challenged everyone in the room to write their own bit of history, and the right kind of history. He was in no doubt the Springboks would win and he announced this to the squad. He believed in them and told them that an entire country did too.

He didn't speak for long. His message to the squad took a few minutes to deliver but it was a message that would stay with the team until the final whistle because they weren't about to play England for the World Cup, they were about to play for the hope of a country and a story that would forever be told and retold.

Typical of how everything had flowed during the World Cup, President Ramaphosa's visit also flowed into the structured morning schedule. It all happened so naturally. Look, if the circumstance had not allowed for it, the president would have been accommodated whenever he had arrived, but the stars just seemed so aligned, even with his visit, which dovetailed so timeously with the day's preparations.

After greeting the team, the president went into the team dining room, followed by the squad. I called Jesse and Trevor to the dining room and their surprise arrival was met with great excitement from everyone.

Jesse and Trevor's smiles were matched only by the smiles of the rest of the players when they saw their two teammates were back in Japan, with Eben beaming the most of all. Getting Jesse and Trevor back was down to Eben's determination that they wouldn't miss out and, of course, Gavin Varejes financially making it possible.

President Ramaphosa made a point of singling out Jesse and Trevor and he invited them to sit with him for brunch. The president said he was so happy that they were in Japan for the final and while he asked about their anguish and disappointment at having been injured, he focused on what a special day he believed it was going to be for the country.

There was such good energy among the squad and such an appreciation for the moment. No one was rushed when catching up with Jesse and Trevor and no one appeared anxious or in any way frantic.

Usually, Charles Wessels, in his capacity as operational manager, JJ Fredericks, the logistics manager, and myself would visit the match-day venue early in the day to dress up the change room and make it 'home' to the players.

However, World Cups are different in that the forward party can only make one entry to the match-day venue, which meant we couldn't set up early, leave and then return to the stadium. As a result, JJ, Aled Walters (conditioning coach), Zeenat Simjee (dietician) and Rayaan Adriaanse (media manager) had to go ahead to set up and await the arrival of the team, while Charles (who served as the team manager at the World Cup) and myself remained with the squad.

Everything on my list that could be done, was completed.

In my early years with the Springboks, when I was the only woman on tour, I'd always use the downtime on match day to get to a salon and let my hair down. It was my treat for the work done in the week and it was the only time I could switch off, even if it was just for an hour to 90 minutes, and remove myself from the memory of the week that was and any thoughts of the day that was still to come. Over the years, one of the Bok physiotherapists, Rene Naylor, joined me and it became part of our match-day ritual.

On the morning of the World Cup final, everything was in order and I had arranged for a hairdresser to come to the hotel so that Rene and I could make a pleasant start to the day. It was a great way to kick off the day, especially with the imminent arrival of the president. The fact that I could allow myself the break, knowing who was addressing the team a few hours later, was an indication – to myself if not anyone else – that there was nothing to stress about and that I needed to soak up the atmosphere of the day without over-complicating my thinking.

As the complement of women in the management increased, it was always a bonus to be able to do the occasional 'girlie' thing with the likes of Rene – the players could at least see that we still enjoyed those spoils, even though our work environment was spent in the testosterone-driven world of men's rugby.

The players, as we got to know them better over time, would be so sweet in asking us if we had booked our hair appointment, as if just to remind us that it was something we had to do. So much of the time that was spent in their company was work-related and driven by the demands of our portfolio, so their interest in our match-day hair ritual made for a light-hearted diversion

SPRINGBOKS
SPRINGBOK
ABSA
1995
2007
SPRINGBOK
SPRINGBOK

PREVIOUS PAGE: With Siya, 'William' and Shaun Seeliger at the Bok hotel in Tokyo.
ABOVE: My good friend, England operations manager Fran Leighton.
TOP RIGHT: Frans looks on as I take a swig from the Webb Ellis Cup.
RIGHT: Bok physio Rene Naylor was my World Cup wingwoman.

SPRINGBOKS

ABOVE: Makazole and Lukhanyo in East London on the Trophy Tour.
TOP RIGHT: Beast shows off the Webb Ellis Cup to his son, Wangu.
RIGHT: Kwagga was a big hit in Japan!

CHAMPIONS
20 19

16
15
ラグビーワールドカップ2019
#RWC2019
RUGBY

ABOVE: Taking a selfie with Makazole in Shizuoka.
TOP RIGHT: With World Cup liaison Sayuri Shida and Bok team manager Charles Wessels.
RIGHT: Watching the Boks beat Namibia with Zeenat, Tanu, Duane and Faf.

CUP
COMPETITION

THE WORLD IN UNION

ABOVE: Hanging out with Bok wives Sarah Louw, Jandré Koch, Ezel Vermeulen and Linca Steyn.
TOP RIGHT: Sitting in the stands at Tokyo Stadium before the quarter-final against Japan.
RIGHT: Tokyo street dining with John, Shimmy and Bryan.

グビーワールドカップ2019

の
基
基

ABOVE: With interpreter Josh Westbrook and assistant liaison Yoshi Enoka in Kobe.
TOP RIGHT: A sushi demo with the kykNET crew.
RIGHT: The Bok wives before the World Cup semi-final against Wales.

ABOVE & TOP RIGHT: Flashing those medals with Sarah and Flo, and Duane and Ezel.
RIGHT: Sipping champagne with Marise Pollard.

WORLD CUP

SPRINGBOK

ABOVE: Bok fans came out in full force for the Trophy Tour in Joburg.
TOP RIGHT: Cup's up with Zeenat and Tanu in Port Elizabeth.
RIGHT: A warm welcome in Shizuoka before our match against Italy.

STRONGER TOGETHER
STRONGER TOGETHER
STRONGER TOGETHER
JAPAN2019

WELCOME CEREMONY
ラグビー南アフリカ代表 歓迎セレモニー
MTN
MTN
MTN
STRONGER TOGETHER

ABOVE: My favourite photo with 'William'.
TOP RIGHT: Getting a sushi lesson in Kagoshima.
RIGHT: A school visit in Tokyo.

ABOVE: About to board the team bus with Sayuri.
RIGHT: Sorting out visas before leaving for Japan.

TOP LEFT: Suitcases for Africa before departure!
BOTTOM LEFT: Players contractual jersey-signing.
ABOVE: Gazing out on Tokyo Bay from my hotel room.

VICTOR MATFIELD
MORNE STEYN
PAT LAMBIE
RUAN PIENAAR
SCHALK BRITS

JAPAN

OPPOSITE PAGE (clockwise from top left): Player luggage tags; allocating World Cup final tickets at the World Rugby offices; the press conference before the final; Bok ladies!
ABOVE: Jesse holding Franco's daughter, Jemi-Mílja Mostert, at Yokohama Stadium.

MTN

CHAMPION

MTN

OPPOSITE PAGE: Our Rugby Championship triumph in Salta, Argentina, set us up perfectly for the World Cup.
ABOVE: All smiles from the Mbonambi family in Japan.

ABOVE: Celebrating Rassie's birthday on the day we arrived home from the World Cup.
TOP RIGHT: Enjoying a Japanese tea-drinking ceremony with Rene.
RIGHT: Looking after 'William' on the Trophy Tour.

TOP: My brother Mike and sister-in-law Helen attended the World Cup semi-final.
ABOVE: Megan, Helen, Izy, Max and Mike before the game.
TOP RIGHT: Family in the stands.
BOTTOM RIGHT: My dad Peter was always my biggest inspiration.

ABOVE: Max, Helen and Izy during the Trophy Tour in Port Elizabeth.
TOP RIGHT: Mike and Max's turn to pose with the cup.
BOTTOM RIGHT: Max and his friend James on the bus with the Boks.

SPRINGBOKS
SPRINGBOKS
RUGBY WORLD CUP

ABOVE: Introducing my mom, Penny, to 'William'.

in conversation. It may not seem like much when written like this, but it was very touching each time they showed they cared.

One of the questions I was often asked throughout the years was what it was like to be a woman in the world of Springbok men's rugby, and it is a credit to the South African players, coaches and fellow management that I never felt singled out, or out of place, because of my gender.

The loneliness in the early days was more about me coming to grips with the portfolio and the squad getting used to having a woman on tour and constantly part of the team environment.

I always felt like the players and coaches treated me with respect, which was down to the way they saw my portfolio within the management. Every person who came into the management was considered to be the best in their field and was identified and offered the position because of the quality of their work. Each time there was a change in coach, there invariably was a change in some management positions, but fortunately I was the one constant throughout, even though I never took it as a given that I would keep my position every time a new coach was appointed.

I was privileged to work alongside Dr Sherylle Calder, who was the visual skills coach and a world leader in her field. She had been part of Clive Woodward's World Cup-winning England squad in 2003 and was very influential in improving the visual skills of the Springbok players in the successful 2007 World Cup campaign. Sherylle served as a specialist on Jake White's management team and was exceptional. A global leader in her field, the feedback from the players in media interviews was a tribute to her skill set. They often mentioned her and I remember Bryan Habana and Jean de Villiers speaking glowingly of how she had added a dimension to their game under the high ball, be it receiving or chasing kicks, and increased their peripheral vision awareness.

Sherylle also added a dynamic within the management because of her experience with the England team and, in some ways, I drew on her confidence and backed myself with more conviction. She was a reminder of each of us being the best in our fields, otherwise we wouldn't be part of the squad.

The first few years of touring with the Springboks had many a lonely moment, which was down to circumstance and nothing to do with the players or other management. I was simply the only woman in the mix and I don't think anyone quite knew back then how to navigate that when on tour. The players would do their thing during their off-time and in a male-dominated environment my exclusion socially would not come from a place of malice. I just don't think it was ever considered that I may want to trek along to wherever it was, even if it was just for a coffee.

It changed pretty quickly the more I got to know the players and the more settled I became. From a management point of view, I felt my voice became stronger when Jake took over in 2004 as he encouraged each one in the management to be the boss of their own portfolio and speak up. What I learned from Sherylle was in the way she professionally owned her portfolio and made no apologies for being as good as she was.

Our portfolios were admittedly very different and I was there to serve the players in a very different way, but I took a lot of good from how Sherylle backed herself and her knowledge of what she had been brought into the squad to share with the players. She never thought of herself as a woman in a man's world, and neither did I. We both always just focused on our portfolios as the reason we were there, and that was the same for Rene when she joined the Springboks in 2008 as a physiotherapist.

More women would follow, among them sports massage therapist Daliah Hurwitz, physiotherapist Dr Tanushree Pillay and Zeenat. Daliah was no longer with the Springboks in 2019 but she was very much a part of our journey, and she would have been as surprised as we were in how much fuss the media in Japan made over the fact that there were four women in the Springbok management. None of us ever thought of it as a big deal, but it felt good to be made aware that many saw us as an inspiration and that there were women who had been inspired to follow our career path because they had seen it was possible.

Globally there had been a lot of media awareness around gender equality, regardless of work profession, but I felt it really was heightened around the time of the 2019 World Cup. World Rugby had made huge strides to advance the women's game, there was constant discussion about equality in the way the men and women players were treated, and there definitely was an increase in female media commentators, reporters, journalists and analysts, which tended to be a media story in itself.

I know from my own experience, and from two decades of working with the Springboks, that the players didn't differentiate between a female and male reporter during an interview. It wasn't something that was ever spoken about because it was never an issue. Rugby was all that mattered to the players and if they were speaking about rugby, the gender of who they were speaking to was irrelevant.

Every Bok squad I worked with had its own dynamic and a lot of it would depend on the success of the squad and the personalities of the players. Things also worked in cycles and a lot depended on the schedule, time spent away from home and who was coaching the team, but the Bok experience of the 2019 World Cup was made that much more pleasurable because of the constant presence of the wives, partners, kids and, near the end, the extended family.

I was always very close to the wives and partners, and got to know all the kids very well over the years, with some of the little ones back in the day now professional rugby players. Who knows, there may be a few of the little ones from 2019 who will be Springboks in the next 20 years.

I enjoyed the company of Siya's wife, Rachel. Like Roxy (John Smit's wife), she is a leader of people and a person of action. Rachel got on with it and helped wherever and whenever she could. She was always willing to do that bit extra to make my life easier, and Handré Pollard's wife, Marise, is very similar. The two made it a lot easier for me on the day of the World Cup final when it came to the logistical finishing touches. They took charge of the wives, partners and kids, in terms of rounding up everyone and ensuring there was some kind of order once everyone arrived at the ground.

The family group on the 2019 World Cup final day was the biggest I'd experienced in all my World Cup tournaments – there were 97 who had to be transported to the stadium on two separate buses. I was there to ensure they all got on the bus, with their tickets and passes, and would communicate by text and WhatsApp with Rachel, Marise and Elmare (wife of then-Bok defence coach Jacques Nienaber) to make sure there were no hiccups once the buses had arrived at the stadium.

The afternoon of the 2019 World Cup final was also unlike any I had ever experienced with the Springboks. Given the enormity of the occasion, the lack of tension among the players underlined how important it was that the wives and partners were so well accommodated in all of the planning.

One of the overriding memories for me on the Saturday afternoon of the final was the image of Franco Mostert and his eldest daughter Joi-Belle, who was dressed in a pink tutu and a Springbok jersey with 'Mostert' printed on the back. She looked adorable and Franco, as ever, was the doting dad. Not far from them in the hotel foyer was Franco's wife Juan-Ri and their little one Jemi-Mílja. They were a typical family enjoying life on a typical Saturday afternoon, but this was no typical afternoon because it was the World Cup final afternoon, and that is exactly what made it so special and so indicative of everything we had got right by making the players' families part of the journey. The players, on the morning of the final, were as close to their home environment as they could have been and looked happy and relaxed.

The family buses left for the ground an hour before the squad buses and the players spent most of the late morning with their loved ones before switching into work mode in the early afternoon to prepare for the game on the world's biggest stage.

Many years ago, I watched a documentary of Clive Woodward's England team just before they left for the hotel to play Ireland in Dublin in a match that would decide the Six Nations. The footage showed Clive talking to the squad, which was captained by Martin Johnson, and it struck me how relaxed everyone was – it was like they were sitting at a pub on a Sunday afternoon. Clive ended by telling his team that, when they walked to the bus, many people would wish them luck. He paused and then said that while those supporters meant well, it was important the players realised they didn't need luck to beat Ireland, what they needed was to play to their ability and they would win. He told the players they had prepared well and now they just had to play well.

I had been in Springbok team meetings on the afternoon of a Test match and it wasn't quite the same experience, but Japan 2019 mirrored what I had seen in that documentary, with the Bok coaches, management and players at peace with their preparation and excited by the occasion. There was so much anticipation and no trepidation and Rassie set the tone in how he spoke and how he acted throughout the World Cup. He was no different on the afternoon of the final to how he was on the afternoon of the opening match.

Charles, meticulous with his operational planning, had factored in the time from the hotel to the stadium, which could take anything from 45 to 90 minutes, and he planned for the longest trip so as not to put the players under any unnecessary stress. The squad buses would leave earlier than was normal because he had planned for any hiccup, given that in Japan there were no police escorts for teams travelling to the stadium on match day.

Thanks to Charles' attention to detail and insistence that he'd rather give players an extra half-hour in the change room than be stuck in traffic, we arrived at the stadium early, with the trip taking 60 minutes.

It would prove so significant because what we didn't know when we arrived at the stadium was that England had miscalculated their departure and would arrive 30 minutes late. It was a frantic scramble for the England players to get on the field for their pre-match warm-up as captain Owen Farrell rushed to make it in time for the coin toss.

Victor Matfield – Bok captain and centurion

Who is Annelee Murray? The mother of the Boks, grandma to the Boks' kids, friend to the Boks' wives and, most important, the one who all of us could trust with the most important things in our lives.

I remember starting at the Boks. Annelee was really like a mother to all of us. Everything was always sorted and in place. We didn't have to worry about anything in our lives when we were in camp. Things were so easy in camp that, whenever we were home, our partners got upset because we were so used to Annelee doing everything for us!

But, as we grew up and got married and then kids arrived, Annelee became more. She became a close friend to all of us and a friend and mother to our wives. It wouldn't be strange to see Annelee at a hotel pushing a pram and having a baby on her hip. She did whatever was needed to make sure that everything was perfect and the players could just focus on the job at hand, and that was to focus on the game on Saturday.

The friendships grew, especially with those of us who were with the Boks for a few years. There wouldn't be a wedding that Annelee wasn't invited to. I think about a trip to New York where Monja and myself met up with Annelee and, of course, because she is so well-travelled, we met her at one of the best restaurants and had the best time, and we left there with places to go to because she knew all the best spots to visit in New York.

Annelee was always there just to make sure we were happy. There were so many times that we, as players, didn't always want to follow the rules of the coaches when they got nervous and maybe a little crazy, but Annelee was always there to help us organise a great day to go and relax and get our heads away from the game.

On the Thursday before the 2007 World Cup final, we wanted to go play golf like we did every Thursday, but Jake said it was not allowed before a game. Of course, Annelee was the one to go organise the best course in Paris. She even organised for our security guards to drive us to the course and back!

Annelee started off as our mother in the Bok camp but grew into a friend and someone we knew would always be there for us and our families.

Chapter 5

OLD FAITHFUL AND THE BIG EASY

Everyone I bumped into at the Yokohama Stadium was giving me the thumbs up, but the most significant voice was that of Jake White. I had seen him earlier in the tournament at our match against the All Blacks, and left our chat feeling despondent and a bit depressed.

I had asked him whether he thought we were going to beat New Zealand and Jake, as always, was straight to the point: 'No.' He said that, even though we wouldn't beat the All Blacks in Yokohama, it would prove to be a good thing for us as he believed South Africa would win the World Cup.

'You are not winning tonight,' said Jake. 'But you will win the final.'

I can't remember if Jake had mentioned who we would be playing in the final, but he seemed adamant that the Springboks would get stronger as the tournament progressed. He seemed to think that an early defeat against the defending champions wasn't a bad thing, but that wasn't why he felt we wouldn't win. He just didn't think we were quite ready to beat them on that particular night, but he wasn't convinced the All Blacks could go all the way. He did say it was going to be some match and he wasn't wrong about that one.

I now hoped that Jake would be as accurate with his prediction of the final as he had been in calling our match against New Zealand. Jake was very upbeat and he reminded me of our chat before the All Blacks match.

'Hey,' he joked when giving me a hug. 'What did I say to you? Didn't I say you'd lose to the All Blacks and win the World Cup?'

The Ice Maiden in me was still strong, as the match hadn't yet started, and I sought reassurance from Jake who seldom got it wrong when it came to calling matches.

'Do you think?' was my obvious response. 'We haven't played yet.'

'Of course,' he said. 'The Boks will be too good tonight.'

It was all I had to hear and, momentarily, I was buzzing with the news that if Jake had called a win, then it was going to be a win. He had also called our quarter-final exit against Australia in New Zealand in 2011, so who was I to doubt him? The man who had coached the Springboks to the World Cup title against England in 2007 was confident there would only be one winner, and it was South Africa.

I was feeling even better about our prospects in the final than when we had left the team hotel, and back then I was convinced we were going to win. Rassie Erasmus, as I've said, was very clear that each person in the management understood their role and that no one got in the way of any others, but he also left it up to each of us to make a contribution to the general well-being of the situation on match days. If the team doctor, masseur, physiotherapist, logistics manager or media manager needed anything, those of us whose portfolio responsibilities had been taken care of just slotted in. If there was a bottle to be filled, a towel to be soaked in cold water for when the players came in at half-time or a query to be answered, whoever wasn't busy got on with it. There were no sacred cows in this management team and it was the same with those players not in the match 23. If there was something to be done, there was always someone in the front of the queue to get it done.

Where I could help, I did. Where a player could help, he did, like when Franco Mostert's wife Juan-Ri was caught in the crowd chaos of trying to get to her seat, just as the anthems were about to be played, and her baby daughter, Jemi-Mílja was in her arms. Both mother and baby looked distressed and I leaned across, took Jemi from her and passed her down to Jesse Kriel, who then proceeded to hold her while singing the national anthem. It was another incredible moment that demonstrated the unity in the squad and just how much of a family we were. It all happened so fast and it appeared frantic, but just knowing Jemi was OK, calmed both Juan-Ri and myself. There was even time to take a photo of Jesse and Jemi. It was a beautiful moment. (The photo, which is in this book, will melt your heart.)

That brief flurry of angst I felt in getting Jemi safely to Jesse was about as hectic as it got for me in the pre-match build-up at the stadium. Charles' planning meant our players were so relaxed in getting to the stadium, having time to settle in the change room and being ahead of schedule for the on-field warm-up.

I had bumped into so many regulars who always attended Bok matches and they were as positive as Jake about the result. When I walked past

Karl Te Nana, the former New Zealand Sevens specialist turned analyst, he shouted out to me that it was going to be a victory for South Africa and the southern hemisphere. The Kiwis I chatted to at the ground were all backing the Springboks and even the Australians were feeling green and gold, even if it wasn't their brand of gold and green.

George Gregan, one of my favourite Australian players, is another of those big-game voices I listen to, and I had a brief chat with him at the stadium. He didn't blink in telling me it was all going to be OK, and that the Springboks would have a good day.

George was one of the best scrumhalves to play the game and he had played the Springboks 30 times in his 139-Test career. He had won 14 times, lost 15 times and drawn once, so if anyone could speak with authority about playing against the Springboks, it was George. I also just enjoyed his energy and attitude. I consider him one of the really good guys and he was a player who commanded respect within the Bok change room and socially he was popular with a lot of the players, even more so after his retirement.

I had got so many text messages from former colleagues and coaches, including the 2007 World Cup winners wishing me the best and telling me to go easy on my whisky flask during the match, because I'd need to have some left to celebrate the win afterwards.

The story of the whisky flask dates back right to the beginning of my Springbok journey, when I would keep a little flask in my inside pocket for the express purpose of calming the nerves during the 80 minutes of the match. I love a single malt whisky and the flask was my go-to on several occasions over the course of 20 years; there was even a time when I was convinced the flask had an impact on the fortunes of the Springboks. It was my prized possession on match day, both in taste and superstition, and at one stage it went missing. I was convinced it had something to do with a succession of Springbok defeats and, even though I got another one, it never quite felt the same. But by the time we got to Japan in 2019, the original flask was back in its rightful place, safely tucked away on the inside pocket of my blazer. (Look out for 'old faithful' in the photo section.)

Talking of an 'old faithful', Percy Montgomery is the one player who religiously messaged me on the morning of a Bok Test. One of Monty's most endearing qualities is his humility as a person and his love for the Springboks. I have known a lot of players and they all love the Springboks, but Monty just seemed to love the Boks that little more.

Monty was the first Springbok Test centurion but if you met him you would think he's just a fanatical Bok supporter. He never speaks about himself, all of his Springbok records or what he has done as a player. Even during the time when he was the Bok kicking and skills coach between 2009 and 2011, he would see himself as a newbie in the management team and not as a player with 102 Tests.

Monty had a very unique experience in going from being the most capped Test Springbok in the squad, to being the newest and most inexperienced member of management. In 2008, he played his 102nd and final Test in a then-record 53-8 win against Australia at Emirates Airline Park (Ellis Park). The players carried him from the field on their shoulders and, just a few months later, Monty walked back into the team room as part of management. For me it was incredible to watch this legend of Springbok rugby be so modest and respect the hierarchy and team ethos of player and management.

I had similarly been amazed when Dr Uli Schmidt was part of the Springbok management under Rudolf Straeuli in 2003. Uli had been an iconic player and a Springbok who would have played many more Test matches had it not been for South Africa's international isolation, but he also embraced his role as the team doctor, focused on that and never projected being a player or wanting to again be that Springbok player in the team environment.

Ray Mordt, a brilliant wing for the Springboks in the early 1980s, was also like that when he was the Bok defence coach in 2002 and 2003. Ray was there to coach and not relive his glory days of scoring a hat-trick of tries against the All Blacks in New Zealand in 1981. The players responded well to him as a coach, but they were all awed by what he had achieved as a player.

I guess it was the measure of the man that Ray never spoke about his Test performances to the players, but he would answer the many questions the players asked him when it came to that feeling of scoring three tries against the All Blacks in a Test match in New Zealand.

Monty and Uli are vastly different characters but what they inherently shared was an understanding of the Springboks when it came to players and management. While we were one as a squad, we were not one and the same in our skills, yet these two giants of the game, who had been superstars on the field, never looked to their glory days as players in doing their job in management. Both were able to separate the two roles, which says a lot about the strength of character of both men.

Monty's match-day Bok message to me was one of the first to come through on my WhatsApp and it was followed by Smitty, Gary Gold, Dick Muir, Fourie du Preez, Victor Matfield and Bryan Habana. Smitty and Bryan were in Japan and I knew I would see them sometime before or after the final – they were as insistent as Jake that it was going to be South Africa's day.

It was always such a boost for me to get these match-day messages from players of such stature and they always celebrated me being in the Springboks, thanked me for my contribution and wanted the team's success to reflect the work I had put in off the field. It was how they felt about management. There was such an appreciation from the players of the roles of the management and if the team won, they felt they'd given the management a thank you for everything done in the build-up to the Test.

Of all the high-profile Boks supporters, the players' favourite has always been South African golfer Ernie Els (nicknamed 'The Big Easy'). It didn't matter who was playing for South Africa, who we were playing against or where we were playing, Ernie and his wife Liezl were always interested in the outcome, always sent messages of support and always made the effort to connect, either by text, voice mail, video or, when Ernie could, in person.

The players adored Ernie and he commanded such a presence whenever he visited the team hotel or popped into the change room after a Test. After beating England one year when Ernie had handed out the jerseys and then joined us after the match for a drink, Adriaan Strauss ranked meeting Ernie as one of the highlights of the season. It turned into a very late, and fun, night.

There was such a regard for what Ernie had achieved in the golfing world as a player and there has always been support from the Springboks for his ambassadorship and funding of the Els for Autism Foundation which offers programmes for those suffering from autism.

Throughout my 20 years of being with the Springboks, Ernie was always Ernie, and it didn't matter which generation of player came into the squad, the questions were always the same: Would Ernie be at the Test and, if so, would there be a chance to meet him?

And when these players did meet Ernie or talk to him, they were always awed by the experience because he is so grounded as a person and so consistent in his support of the Boks because it has never been based on the result. I knew that, win or lose the final, I'd have Ernie on the phone wanting to speak to Duane, Siya, Rassie and the players, either to congratulate them or to remind them that their focus had to be on the next match.

Ernie was playing in a tournament in Asia over the World Cup final weekend and couldn't be at the match. While we made every effort to align his and the team's travel schedules for after the World Cup, it just wasn't possible and on this occasion Ernie's presence would have to be through a video call after the final.

Earlier in the tournament we had also received a personalised video message via Johann Rupert from legendary NFL quarterback Tom Brady, who is a favourite amongst the players, especially Lood de Jager and Handré Pollard, who follow American football.

I would have thought the hour before the World Cup final would be the most nerve-racking for the players, but it was remarkable how considered and calm they were, which was in contrast to England's players, who had arrived late at the stadium.

We had heard they were stuck in traffic and at one stage there were even whispers that the match start could be delayed, which thankfully it wasn't because it would have felt like we were punished for getting it right and they were rewarded for getting their timing wrong.

Our players were focused and intense in the pre-final warm-up, but as I keep on stressing, they were just so in control of their emotions and time. The schedule structure was their guide and every minute was accounted for in the build-up to the first whistle. Each player and squad member knew exactly what had to be done in the countdown to taking the field and while it was a World Cup final, Rassie's message was that it was also a game of rugby, the ritual of which all of them had been through hundreds of times since they first start playing as bare-footed six-year-olds.

His team talks were from the heart and those who have watched the Springboks' World Cup documentary, *Chasing the Sun,* will know exactly what I mean when I refer to the power of his pre-match talks and also the honesty of those talks in the change room at half-time during the tournament.

Rassie's approach, which was all about honesty and empowerment, filtered down to the senior players, who also comfortably spoke from the heart and without restriction in the heat of the moment. There was, to quote him, 'no bullshitting of ourselves'. If we were playing well, there would be an endorsement of that and a reinforcement of what the players had to do in the second half and, if it had been a struggle, then there was no sugar-coating the situation. He told the players exactly what he was thinking and what was needed to fix things.

It was fascinating to be so close to the on-field warm-ups of the two squads. We were well into our routines when the England players started appearing on the field, some in bunches and others individually. They just looked flustered and I don't blame them after being stuck in traffic.

We, as management, had got so much right at the World Cup, and it always took me back to Clive Woodward's speech to the Bok management in 2004. What could we do that would give the player an edge over the opposition or an extra percent for the match? In this instance, Charles' meticulous planning had given us a big mental boost and advantage before kick-off.

I briefly sighted England's coaching duo of Eddie Jones and John Mitchell on the field. They greeted us, but they'd arrived late and their focus was on their players and the warm-up.

John had also said hello to a few of the Springbok players who passed him on their way back to the change room and, on seeing the attitude of our players, John remarked that England could be in for a 'tough old evening'. I doubt even John could ever have imagined just how tough it would get for England, from that first collision that knocked out Kyle Sinckler to the last. I never pictured myself sitting in the stadium medical room for the final 15 minutes of the first half watching Lood and Kyle's dreams of completing a World Cup final being shattered.

I also didn't know that as soon as I got back to the change room at half-time, I'd also get the news that our starting hooker Bongi Mbonambi's final had also ended because of injury. Bongi had come off just after Lood because of a knock to the head and been taken for a concussion test, which he failed.

I had one message to make, which was to Bongi's wife Anastacia to let her know that he wouldn't be returning to the field, but that he would be OK. Bongi's World Cup, like Lood's, was over. But as I was about to discover over the next 40 minutes, the Springboks' World Cup final was just warming up.

Johann Muller – Bok captain

During the years I was involved with the Springboks, I was privileged to have met and worked closely with Annelee.

I immediately realised that the word 'impossible' was not in her vocabulary. If you needed something done and done properly, you would ask Annelee. She did so much more than her job description and nothing was too much effort, whether making extra travel arrangements, looking after our loved ones on game days, or general responsibilities and activities.

Annelee's calmness and support during my captaincy role in New Zealand, under immense pressure and responsibilities, will always be one of my fond memories of her.

Coaches, management and players have changed over the years, but when I think of Annelee's role, I see her as the glue that kept everything together in the Springbok setup. She has a passion for the game of rugby, her job and, most of all, a passion for people.

I always thought with the number and variety of people Annelee has met, things she's seen and experienced, she could write a book. I have no doubt that this book will be honest, insightful and interesting, and I can't wait to read it.

Annelee, thank you for all the good times, your hard work, support and the fun and memories shared.

To me you will always be the ultimate team player!

Chapter 6

LIFE COULDN'T GET MORE PERFECT

Lood de Jager wanted to sit among the substitutes and watch the rest of the final. He was in such pain that it was even a struggle for him to lean over and put on his takkies, so I got down on my knees and put them on for him, and made sure he was as comfortable as possible, with his left shoulder in a sling and his motion of arm movement so restricted.

Lood has this adorable baby face, but there are few tougher players and I don't even want to imagine how uncomfortable the final 30 minutes were for Lood, who in the weeks leading up to the final had spent a lot of time with me to make sure we could get his wife Constance and their little boy Elijah to Japan.

Constance wasn't coming if they couldn't get a visa for Elijah but Lood wanted his wife and son there and nothing was going to stand in his way. Once again, the Japanese Embassy staff were superstars and everything got sorted, but it certainly was a week where it seemed like Lood and I were tied to each other by an umbilical cord. When I think about the 2019 World Cup final, Lood will forever be the first player who comes to mind.

The final, as it was unfolding, was such a blur to me. My adrenaline surged with the kick-off and the rest of the final seemed to play out in the background as I was preoccupied with the injured players.

I am not seat bound during a Test match and I am always on the move, busying myself with whatever I can, so as to try and beat the nerves. In that first half and leading into half-time there wasn't much time to think about the match, but everything seemed to settle in the second half and I was able to watch. I tried but I couldn't, so I was off again, doing my usual rounds of distraction and sending my customary text messages to close friends, including John Smit's wife Roxy who, back when Smitty was captaining the side, was my equal in terms of needing distractions during the game.

If we were playing overseas and Roxy was back in Durban, I'd text her during the game and ask her what she was thinking and whether she was confident we would win. Her favourite response was that she was outside in the garden 'pruning the roses'. She would occasionally check in for the score and then go back to gardening.

At the Yokohama Stadium in 2019, there obviously weren't any roses to prune and there was no Roxy nearby, so I did my walk to the change room, back to the stands and then to the change room again. I would listen for the noise, then check my phone and get a glance of the match. I kept on telling myself it was ridiculous to be this nervous and acting like this. It was a World Cup final, people had paid thousands of dollars for match tickets, millions of South Africans were glued to their television sets and there were times in the second half that I wasn't watching, simply because I couldn't bear the tension.

Midway through the second half, I found myself seated in the change room with our two liaison officers, Yoshi Enoki and Josh Westbrook, who were given a front-row seat to all my nervousness and match-day madness. I couldn't watch, but I wanted to watch. I asked them to put on the television and then watched for a bit and asked them to switch it off, then back on, then off. Then I was texting and then I just made a decision to be brave enough to go and watch the final 20 minutes, after having a sip from my flask.

We seemed in control of the match on the scoreboard, and as I made my way back to the stands the South Africans in the crowd were buoyant and jubilant. All the momentum seemed to be with us, but I never took anything for granted until the final whistle was blown. Then it happened, almost out of nowhere. Makazole Mapimpi ran, kicked the ball ahead for Lukhanyo Am to gather and pass back to 'Mapimps', who scored the first try by a Springbok in a World Cup final. For those who don't know the history of South Africa's World Cup finals, in 1995 the Springboks beat the All Blacks 15-12 in extra time at Ellis Park in Johannesburg and in 2007 the Springboks beat England 15-6 in Paris in France, and despite winning there were no tries scored by either side in those finals. It looked like it was going the same way in Japan when we led 18-12 in the final, but in the 66th minute we scored what will always be an iconic try for the Springboks at the World Cup because it was the first in a final.

Handré Pollard converted and I still didn't believe we were safe at 25-12. I appeared to be the only one with the nerves and the South African fans were in full throttle. I found the familiar face of the match director, Brendan Morris, and he gave me an acknowledgement and a nod that the final was ours. I needed to hear the final whistle before I would believe it.

Then Cheslin Kolbe scored and the big screens at the stadium switched between the player celebrations after his try and the engraving of 'South Africa' on the Webb Ellis Cup. I looked at the clock and there were two minutes to play and we were ahead by 20 points. I glanced back at Brendan and he smiled and said: 'I think you've got this one.'

The relief on hearing that final whistle and the feeling of elation was just so … I don't even know if there is a word that can describe just what I felt in that moment. I rarely cry, but I was crying and the first person I hugged was Lood. We just hugged and cheered. We were world champions. We had won the World Cup.

Smitty, who had been in Japan as an analyst, was on the field and so was Bryan Habana, who was also working as a television analyst for the tournament. Bryan ran up to me and his embrace was so powerful, it could have been a tackle and Smitty was just beaming with pride that the Springboks had won.

Smitty and Bryan are such amazing ambassadors for South Africa and for the Springboks, and the joy that they got from the success of 2019 was no different to the emotion they showed in Paris in 2007 when they won the World Cup. Smitty captained the 2007 World Cup-winning team and Bryan equalled Jonah Lomu's tournament record of eight tries and was named the World Rugby Player of the Year, but in Japan they were fans living in the moment of a Springbok World Cup win.

At one stage I had asked Smitty if he was going to come back to the team hotel later that night or if we would be seeing him in the change room and he just smiled and said 'No Annelee, this is your time, this is Siya's time and this is about the 2019 world champions. Go and celebrate and enjoy yourself. Drink that whisky now.'

It took a very special leader to captain the Springboks after the 2003 World Cup and Smitty was that person. He would win a World Cup in 2007 and end his career as one of a handful of Springbok Test centurions, but his impact on Springbok rugby should never be forgotten. I don't think the fans have ever quite appreciated just how important Smitty was to the Springboks and the 2007 World Cup triumph.

The first person I thought of when the final whistle went was my dad,

Peter, who had passed away earlier in the year. He was my rock and the one who introduced me to rugby and took me to my first big matches in Port Elizabeth. The first time I watched the Springboks was against the British & Irish Lions at Boet Erasmus Stadium in 1980, when it bucketed down with rain and we won thanks to Naas Botha's kicking. I knew my dad would have been so proud of me and I just missed him so much in that moment. I wished he could have been there, experiencing the World Cup win and seeing me be a part of the Springboks and that victory.

It was about as emotional a moment as I have experienced in my 20 years with the Springboks and the first person I texted was my brother. 'We won the World Cup.'

What followed on the field was just one mass celebration of hugs, kisses, high fives and smiles. The players and management couldn't stop grinning and the wives, partners and children were on the field just living this moment with them.

President Ramaphosa was also on the field and sharing in the moment, as he had predicted he would when he spoke to the team 12 hours earlier.

I was so happy for Siya and Rassie, and the man that Siya had become from the shy young man who I first welcomed to the Springboks in 2013.

Siya's leadership style was always all-encompassing and he was always secure enough and strong enough to lean on the experience of players like Duane Vermeulen, Willie le Roux, Eben Etzebeth and the flyhalf general Handré Pollard. Siya made his Test debut against Scotland in 2013 and was named Man of the Match on what was his birthday weekend. Six years later, the World Cup final would be his 50th Test match. It is customary for the team to hang back and allow a player in his 50th or 100th Test to run out on his own to enjoy the applause of the crowd, but Siya refused this honour on the night of the World Cup final because he said the occasion was bigger than his personal milestone and that the Springboks would win the final as a unit and not because of one person. This meant the players walked out onto that field as a unit, not with one person first and then the rest of the squad following 30 seconds later.

As Siya prepared himself to receive the World Cup trophy, I knew this was his moment, one as iconic in South African sporting history as when Nelson Mandela handed over the trophy to Francois Pienaar in 1995. Duane and Pieter-Steph du Toit gently nudged me to the front of the podium because they said I'd be lost at the back.

'You deserve to be there, Annelee,' said Pieter-Steph as I stepped forward just in time for Siya to raise the 'William' to the heavens. Right in that moment, I just wanted time to stand still, because life couldn't get more perfect.

Jean de Villiers – Bok captain and centurion

Growing up, I always wanted to play for the Springboks. When I eventually got selected, I was waiting for the coach or someone to get in touch with me to provide more details as to what I had to do next.

That never happened and rather than the coach I got a message from Annelee Murray. At that stage, I had no idea what she did in the Bok setup, but when I retired 13 years later I could easily say that her value to the team is on par with the head coach – or more!

She's been referred to as the 'mother of the Springboks' and that is very true. I know she doesn't like that title but it's the motherly characteristics that are relevant here – a mother in the way that she cares about the team, players and their families, always putting the Springboks first and playing such an integral part in creating a happy environment for the team to perform.

Whether it's helping the wives and kids on game day, or sorting out a visa (she definitely won't miss the visa struggles!) in no time, I think her job description is impossible to fully explain.

The Boks will miss her, no doubt, but the impact that she had on so many people will last a lifetime!

When becoming a Springbok I didn't know who she was but now that I've left the Springboks it's impossible to forget her. I'm honoured to call her a friend.

Annelee, all the best with life after the Boks. May you enjoy the adventure, travel the world and hopefully the evening whiskies taste better than ever!

Chapter 7

FRANS STEYN AND THE ROYAL CHALLENGE

I had the privilege of walking the World Cup trophy to the post-final media conference and as fate would have it, I bumped into Eddie Jones and Owen Farrell, who had just finished their media conference as the losing side.

Typical of Eddie's dry sense of humour, he glanced at the trophy and said: 'That's not ideal, Annelee.'

In the build-up to the 2019 final, Eddie had told the media that he had experienced both sides of a World Cup final – the ecstasy of winning it with the Springboks in 2007 and the anguish of losing it in 2003 when England's Jonny Wilkinson had kicked an extra-time drop goal to beat the Wallabies. Eddie said that he knew which feeling he wanted to experience in Japan and, as he walked past me, I knew whatever he was feeling was not part of his script. But Eddie is a class act and he gave me a hug and said, 'well done'. I spoke briefly with him later on when he came into the Springbok change room to congratulate the team.

My favourite off-field moment of the night of the World Cup final came when we got back to the change room after the on-field presentation.

Frans Steyn had been tasked with carrying the trophy back into the Springbok change room. As a 20-year-old, he had won the trophy in 2007 in Paris and, 12 years later as a veteran who had played his club rugby almost exclusively in France for the past decade, he had the World Cup in his hands again and was about to deliver it to his teammates. It was one of those Hollywood 'wow' moments and I was thrilled for Frans, who is just such a wonderful person.

I believe anyone who is a Test player can play the game and I think every player who wears the green and gold jersey is good, but throughout my time at the Springboks, the one player who other players always spoke of with a sense of awe was Frans Steyn. He was so talented, so good no matter whether he was playing fullback, wing, centre or flyhalf, and he is pretty unique as a character.

I was there in 2004 when Jake took the Springbok squad to watch Grey College play a schools rugby match in Bloemfontein. It was Jake's first Test in charge and he is never one to miss an opportunity to watch talented young rugby players. But there was a specific reason Jake wanted the Bok players at Grey College that day, and it was Frans Steyn.

'Watch him,' Jake told the players. 'He is going to be your teammate at the 2007 World Cup.'

Jake knew then he was going to pick Frans Steyn as a Springbok and in 2006, the Springboks' centenary year, Frans made his debut for South Africa at Lansdowne Road in Dublin as a winger and was the South African Man of the Match.

It was a very different and youthful looking Frans who sprinted down the wing to score a spectacular try in 2006, and I will forever remember him as a player who always came good in the biggest moments of a game.

Every Springbok player is dear to me, but some just resonated a little more with me than others, and one of those players was Frans. I had watched him grow from a teenager in 2006 into one of the team leaders in 2019, and shared his joy at getting married and being the father to three daughters.

Frans was unbelievable as a player in 2007, but I don't think even he knew just how big winning the World Cup was back then. He kicked a long-distance pressure penalty in the final to go with Monty's four penalties, but for someone who had always succeeded at rugby, it may have been a case of him asking why everyone was fussing. It all came so easy for Frans and he is one player who I always thought would play the most Test matches for South Africa.

Rassie was as big on Frans' qualities as a player as Jake had been in 2006. What was different was that Jake picked a teenager on potential and Rassie entrusted the skills of a veteran to do a particular job for him at the World Cup. One of the biggest squad influences in Japan was the contribution, on the field and off it, of a seasoned players like Frans. Francois Louw and Schalk Brits were two other veterans who added experience and composure, and showed just how good they were after nearly a decade of playing club rugby in England.

The Frans Steyn who won the World Cup in 2019 was very aware how big it was this time because of his 12 years' international experience in between wins. Frans and Os du Randt just happened to be two of those players who I will always have a soft spot for and each of them, schooled in Bloemfontein, won two World Cups, 12 years apart. Their individual stories are amazing and their pedigree as players is equally remarkable.

Os won the World Cup in 1995 and Jake brought him out of retirement in 2004 to win it again in 2007. Rassie did the same with Frans, in never doubting his ability to deliver for the Springboks. Frans had been playing in France but it was only when Rassie took over in 2018 that Frans was permanently back in the Test reckoning.

Frans isn't a person who plays mind games and he respected Rassie's honesty up front. It reminded me of Jake's talks with Monty when he picked him for the Springboks in 2004. Monty had been playing in Wales for three years but Jake immediately wanted him involved with the Boks. He met with Monty and spelt out what his role would be in the team, and also the expectation he had of Monty. Rassie did the same with Frans. I keep on saying it, that although Rassie and Jake may not think they are similar, their Springbok coaching similarities are scary in the best possible way.

Frans walked the World Cup trophy back into the change room at the Yokohama Stadium, and then the celebrations could really start. Eddie did the respectful thing in visiting our change room, but not all the England players came over. I remember a handful being there, with flanker Tom Curry prominent because he swapped his England No 6 jersey with Siya. The Vunipola brothers, Billy and Mako, were also very gracious in coming to congratulate the team.

Outside of the squad, SA Rugby president Mark Alexander, CEO Jurie Roux and head of selectors Pieter Jooste also popped in. There was a very strong and professional relationship with Rassie and Jurie, and there was also an alignment with the executive leadership and the coaches. It made such a difference with everyone pulling in the same direction and just wanting what was best for the Springboks.

Jurie is a well-respected CEO in world rugby but he wasn't someone who hung out with the team or the players unless they had invited him. He entrusted Rassie with rugby matters and backed him to deliver, which was the case in Japan.

The one special guest in the change room was Prince Harry, who applauded the performance and in a short message told the players just how powerful their victory would be for South Africa as a country. Frans (who else?) got

Prince Harry a Heineken beer and, on toasting him, challenged him to down the beer. Harry politely declined, pointing to all the cameras present, by way of cellphones.

Again, I couldn't help but think of 2007 in Paris, and all the similarities in that World Cup win. Harry also figured in 2007, but in a very different way. The prince and his brother William are big England rugby fans and they attended the final in Paris. It so happened that when the players were walking back to the team bus just after midnight, given the late kick-off in Paris, Smitty spotted the two princes. As only Smitty would do, he approached them and asked for a photo with the two of them. They sheepishly agreed, but didn't seem overly impressed at the Bok captain's request. I think they were hurting a lot from the defeat.

Fast forward 12 years and Prince Harry was no longer a youngster, and when he came to congratulate the Boks it was in a different guise and with a very different persona. The players loved his visit but the highlight was always going to be Ernie Els, who couldn't be at the match but was not going to miss out on any of the celebrations.

Ernie called me on FaceTime and politely asked me to point the camera at the players, the room and the festivities so that he could get a sense of the party. I don't know who or how many players he spoke with, but he spent a while on the phone congratulating them and the coaches on the win. With Ernie in conversation with the World Cup-winning Boks it was 2007 all over again (Ernie had been at the Paris final and was very much part of the festivities afterwards).

The only person missing in 2019 in Japan was the late Madiba, but even though he physically wasn't present, his spirit was never far away from any Springbok occasion.

Schalk Burger – Bok captain

Annelee ... Where to start? Well, we met in 2003. Me, young and lost in a Springbok setup less than ideal for a youngster, out of place in a very foreign environment, craving knowledge and information of what is required of me and what to do.

And that's where I met Annelee. But she was already providing guidance to many of the senior Springboks of that era, so what chance did I stand of getting the same treatment as some of the more seasoned veterans? Turns out, every chance.

I didn't need to worry because that's just who Annelee is. You ask a question and you get help or, if she can't help you, she puts you in touch with someone who can.

If there is an issue, she takes it upon herself to deal with it and you never hear of it again.

I think all of us who worked closely with her over a long period of time have got the utmost respect for the undoubted mother of the Springboks.

I fear that these words don't do her justice, nor does my writing to try and put my gratitude on paper.

Without the help of Annelee in 2004, my then-girlfriend, now-wife, would never have made it to my first Test match at Newlands.

I had asked how our partners must get to the stadium. Annelee explained they all arrive at The Cullinan hotel and from there the shuttle will take them to and from the game. My reaction was, 'But she doesn't have her driver's licence yet and she lives in Stellenbosch.'

Rest assured, Annelee got it all sorted out for me.

From babysitting me in Sydney in 2003, where we basically lived at the BokTown, to becoming best of friends for myself and my family.

Please never stop taking us to the latest culinary hotspots in Cape Town and most of all, let's keep sharing good bottles of wine!

Oh, and after all these years, even though I am retired and nearly 40, Annelee is still looking after me like she did back in 2003.

Thank you for everything.

Chapter 8

HARRY PUT ME IN MY PLACE

When I look back to 2001, in my very first home Test, it was so different to my last Test in Japan. For starters, we won in Japan in a final so many said we couldn't win, while in 2001 we lost a Test match at a venue where so many felt we couldn't lose, and against a team of French youngsters not given any chance of beating the Springboks.

In the aftermath of having opened the 2001 season with a loss against France in Johannesburg, Springbok backline coach Tim Lane had in jest suggested that someone should have taken a mallet to the stadium floodlights at Ellis Park after Breyton Paulse's try 27 seconds into the match. Tim had said that because it never got better for us than in those first 27 seconds, and we lost a Test everyone believed we would win comfortably.

Everyone, that is, except Tim who had cautioned the South African players that the young French team playing at Ellis Park was the best in France and that the youngsters were the form players.

Tim didn't think the Springboks would lose, but having just finished coaching Clermont in the French Top 14, he knew how tough the Test would be, and he wasn't wrong. France won and it proved to be a baptism of fire for me because the Test match week in South Africa is very different when the Springboks lose.

Structurally and operationally nothing changes, but the attitudes definitely change. All the hype and positivity of the six-week training camp in Plettenberg Bay quickly got lost in the following week when the public relations intensified, the media turned on us and the Springboks were in survival mode, just one week into their season.

In the next 20 years, the only country in which I experienced a similar knee-jerk reaction to their team losing was in New Zealand, when the All Blacks lost a Test, and that wasn't too often. In South Africa, more so in the early 2000s than now, the media treated players as if losing was a crime, punishable by firing squad, and there was no softening in the media hammering or even acknowledgement that perhaps the other team just happened to be better.

The reaction in the media was always along the lines that the Springboks did not lose at home, even though history will tell you that they did. For Springbok coach Harry Viljoen defeat wasn't an option because he was not going to be done any favours by the media, many of whom were angry at him for investing in Australian coaches – they felt he was too Australian in his rugby thinking and too business-like in his approach. Harry needed time to change the way of thinking among the Springboks and the South African rugby public, but in 2001 time was a luxury he wasn't going to get from the rugby media or those doubters within South African rugby's corridors, where there was a division in their support of his appointment and also because of the Australian coaches and consultants he had contracted to the Springboks.

These days many international teams have foreign coaches and foreigners in management, as we did in 2019 with Felix Jones and Aled Walters, but in 2001 Harry was ahead of his time, and the situation never played out as he had imagined it would.

Harry is a very successful businessman and he wanted a more business-like approach, from the management and the players. He spoke a sporting business language back then that was probably 10 years too early for the players because, as much as they all bought into Harry's business vision for the Springboks and his rugby philosophy, very few could translate the words into action.

There were more perceived failures than successes and while there were individual exceptions, Harry in 2001 was constantly having to convince players that there was another way of doing things and a more professional way of conducting themselves, on and off the field.

Harry wanted to change the perception that the Springboks were physically imposing and a team that relied on their brawn more than their brains. He encouraged players to have an opinion and to think and challenge each other. He wanted them to learn from other sporting codes in Australia and the United States, and he used professional franchises in the latter as the yardstick of what he wanted to achieve with the Springboks and in South African rugby. I am a big fan of American sports and professionally over the years I got a lot of inspiration from how they did it at the biggest franchises in the United States, whether it was basketball, NFL, ice hockey or baseball. I was fortunate over the years to have the resources to travel to the States and visit clubs and franchises. Their public relations people were always willing to accommodate me and share their knowledge with me. I know I gained a lot and took a lot into the Springbok environment because of those private visits to the USA.

It was easy for me to relate to Harry's excitement when he spoke about the standards of professionalism in the American sports and that it was a standard he wanted the Springboks to achieve, but on reflection he was just someone so ahead of his time in South African sport.

It was thrilling to be a part of Harry's thinking and the coach had the full backing of SA Rugby CEO Rian Oberholzer, who had employed me in 2000 and created a public relations portfolio that allowed me to split my time between SA Rugby and the Springboks.

Rian, who remains a mentor and inspiration to me today, encouraged me to apply my corporate knowledge and experience in making a difference to the way things had been done within the Springboks and SA Rugby in terms of the VIP match-day experience and the general perception of the Springboks and SA Rugby.

I had replaced Lisa Bon (now Kingi-Bon) who was moving to New Zealand. Lisa and I have always kept in touch, compared notes, grown in our professional careers and maintained the strongest of bonds. My role was different to Lisa's at SA Rugby, but she was a big help to me because she had spent a big part of her career in rugby and this was my first experience of working in the sport. Lisa, having worked for SA Rugby for a decade, was snapped up by the New Zealand Rugby Union and settled very easily into life there. She embraced New Zealand as her new home and also the All Blacks as her new team, but she will tell you that there is a part of her that remains a Springbok and she celebrates her South African heritage. Lisa was fabulous in the job she had done for SA Rugby, but where my role differed was that it had been expanded to focus on the Springboks too.

Rian believed in Harry as a coach and part of my job spec was to make Harry's life easier, especially when it came to all the organisational demands that come with being the head coach of the Springboks. Everyone wants a piece of the Bok coach, be it to do talks, fundraisers or have the players do something community- or media-related, and in 2001 the media landscape was so much different because of the absence of social media.

Players and coaches these days are much more empowered because they can dictate accuracy in their message through proper use of their own social media platforms.

It wasn't like that in 2001 when the media often was the making or breaking of a player or coach, with so much determined through perception and not necessarily accuracy in the reporting. In my public relations capacity, I had to accept the realities of the media space and detach myself from the hurt some players felt because of media reports that got very personal. The media never goes away and they are always integral to any Springbok environment, so my focus was on how to educate the players and, where possible, get a better understanding of the media personalities because those individuals were important in taking the message of the players, the team and the sponsors to the greater public.

Harry also had specific ideas about the wives and partners being more closely involved in the squad dynamic and how he wanted me to play a role in breaking down stereotypes that may have existed in the squad when it came to the inclusiveness of family.

When it comes to family inclusiveness and the players' mental health – considering the role of the wife or partner, the well-being of the players' children and being away from family for such lengthy periods – what was second nature to everyone in the 2019 World Cup squad was revolutionary in 2001.

Harry had been out of rugby coaching for a decade, in which time he had focused exclusively on his businesses, but he had a strong friendship with the 1999 World Cup-winning coach Rod Macqueen, who had recommended his backline assistant Tim Lane to Harry. Tim had left the Wallabies after the World Cup to join Clermont in France and he coached the club to the Top 14 final in his first year. The Top 14 final was played one week before Tim's first Test with the Boks, which happened to be against a French team that included many of the players he had coached all season.

Tim arrived in Johannesburg just five days before the Test, although there had been regular interaction with him in the months leading into the Test, as I had to assist with finding him a house in Cape Town, with his wife and children all relocating to South Africa.

Harry had replaced Nick Mallett as Springbok coach for the end-of-year tour in 2000, but 2001 ushered in the Harry Viljoen era which started with great fanfare but ended abruptly when he resigned just one year later.

Rian was very liberal in his thinking and empowered me to improve all areas of South African rugby's public relations and also provide support to Harry and the Springbok management.

Harry, who had enjoyed success in South Africa as a player and a coach with Transvaal (now the Lions), Natal (now the Sharks) and Western Province, had maintained a keen interest in global rugby trends and he was very familiar and impressed with the type of rugby the Wallabies had played in winning the 1999 World Cup.

Harry was an admirer of the Australian backline play and he wanted the best of the Wallabies involved with the Springboks, which is how Tim ended up in South Africa as assistant coach to the Springboks. Harry raved about Tim's philosophy on back play and how it would add a dimension to the Springboks. The Australian influence also included rugby league coaches Frank Ponissi and Les Kiss, as well as the former Aussie rules kicking and skills coach Mick Byrne, who had also coached rugby union in Australia.

Les went on to coach Ulster in Ireland, Frank would win NRL (National Rugby League) titles as general manager at the Melbourne Storm and Mick spent eight years with the All Blacks and won two World Cups in 2011 and 2015. Mick also had a spell with the Wallabies after the All Blacks and I stayed in touch with him over the years. All of them loved their South African experience and they really enjoyed the Springbok players. Even though we didn't immediately get the World Cup-winning benefit in 2003 of this foreign influence, I do believe what Harry started in 2001 contributed to the evolvement of a more professional and liberated Springbok management structure which has become a world leader in rugby over the past 20 years.

It was also the Australian coaches who first remarked on the diversity in the Bok squad and felt that South Africa's diversity would become the team's strength, especially when the game had transformed. Back in 2001, I heard what they were saying, but it was only in 2018 and 2019 that I truly understood what they had meant about the collective power of this diversity.

One of my first Springbok responsibilities in 2001 was, at Harry's request, to do a presentation to selected senior players on the subject of public relations, the image of the team and the individual, what the expectation would be of these senior players and also the importance of the team sponsors and how I proposed to improve the relationship between the squad and the sponsors.

Harry also wanted me to talk about the six-week training camp in

Plettenberg Bay, what we were going to do that was new, how we would embrace the sponsors who had been so loyal to the Springboks and how better to communicate with Springbok supporters.

I was so nervous about standing up and speaking to a room full of these South African rugby icons, with Mark Andrews, André Venter and Joost van der Westhuizen being three of the names on the list who had been flown to Cape Town.

Harry's adviser and the team's communications manager, Mark Keohane, met me downstairs at what was then the Cape Sun in Strand Street and he gave me details of the morning and when I would be speaking. I told him I was so nervous and he said it would be OK and I needed to think of breathing into a paper bag, as it would calm any nerves.

He said the players were people, like me, and that they were all good guys and that there was no reason to be nervous. He said they would be interested in what I had to say, as they wanted to have a better image and a stronger relationship with the sponsors and I was there to guide them in achieving those things.

I can't say I ever lost that nervousness when speaking to the players over the course of 20 years, but no occasion was ever quite as daunting as that first one. It went well and the players were great in listening and then asking questions that were very specific to all the areas I felt needed improving but which were dependent on the players' buy-in. They showed a genuine interest in the sponsors and the professional business of rugby and sponsorships.

One of my focus areas was in growing the relationship between the sponsor, associate sponsor and the team, and explaining to the players the differences in sponsors of the Springboks and sponsors at the provinces and regions, in terms of their marketing objectives.

There was a lot of education required around the kit sponsor, who at the time was Nike. Players in their personal capacity can be sponsored by various brands but footwear is carved out of the contract as it is an individual preference and can affect performance.

For the rest, there were strict protocols with the Springboks' team sponsor when in camp and on tour. Some players would test the boundaries, turning their socks inside out to hide the national sponsorship branding, or strategically use tape to cover the national sponsor logo in support of their provincial or personal sponsors.

I was aware of why they were doing it, but it was not going to be tolerated and the best way to teach someone is to educate them as to why they had a national responsibility to those sponsors who were the lifeblood of the sport and invested heavily in the Springboks and rugby in South Africa. The players came to understand that it wasn't a case of choosing sides between rival provincial and national sponsors, they were to support both based on which camp they were in or which tournament they were playing in at any given time. What we were demanding of them at a national level was exactly what was expected of them when they returned to their provinces.

I enjoyed the presentation to the players and was surprised at the depth of their questions, but it was revealing how underappreciated some players said they felt, how they believed so little was being done for the partners and wives, and just how much they wanted to feel cared for outside of the Test results. They wanted some love and they wanted their wives, partners and children to feel special as part of the extended Springbok family.

Harry was all for me doing whatever I could to make them feel valued and to make their partners feel as much a part of the Test match experience. It was the start of everything we had as a squad in 2019, which had been 20 years in the making.

When I first joined the Boks, partners sat in the stands during matches. I fought hard for a suite which has pretty much become the norm and makes life so much easier for the players who have young kids.

The players' questions also helped shape a lot of my focus areas for the duration of the six-week camp in Plettenberg Bay where I was first introduced to the leadership at the old Southern Sun, which is now Tsogo Sun. Hazel Lewis was the go-to person and she managed the Springboks account on a daily basis, while the executives John van Rooyen, Neil Fraser and, in later years, Ravi Nadasen were unbelievable in how they always put the needs of the players and management first. They turned the Southern Sun/Tsogo Sun into a home away from home for the squad and they remained a constant partner in my 20 years with the team. Team jersey sponsors changed, tournament sponsors came and went and associate sponsors also worked in cycles, but what was always there like a caring and loving parent was the hotel group leadership. Though they changed from Southern Sun to Tsogo Sun, the name changed and the partnership grew in strength. The players loved staying at the same hotels in each city and they had their favourites throughout the years, in which they would build, in some cases, lifelong friendships with the staff from all around South Africa.

I am biased but I'd like to think that the staff thought of the Springboks as their favourite sporting team.

The players always appreciated what was done for them at home and when we were overseas they'd often compare the quality of service to what they received in South Africa, and we stayed in some of the finest hotels overseas and got five-star treatment. The players pining for The Cullinan hotel, the Palazzo or the Beverley Hills in Umhlanga was more of a compliment to those who accommodated them in South Africa than it was an insult to their overseas hosts.

Our boys were spoilt and they knew it. It was the same with one of the early airline partners, British Airways/Comair, and the account executive Charlie Newell, who became as much of a legend among the players as SA Breweries' Rob Fleming. Charlie and Rob set a standard that made the players believe in the integrity of the sponsor. Nothing was too much for Charlie and over the years he arranged many flights and accommodation packages for the players, management and respective families – in which he would always get them the best possible deal. Thank you, Charlie.

Rob is a rugby lover and can sit for hours and just discuss and debate the game. He was a big supporter of the Springboks and was motivated in wanting the relationship to be very special. SA Breweries, through Castle Lager, had always been synonymous with rugby, soccer and cricket in South Africa. The players' life view was something along the lines of, 'you braai, you drink Castle Lager and you watch the Springboks, Proteas or Bafana play.'

Rob was among the sponsors who spent time with the squad in Plettenberg Bay and the interaction between him and the players really put down a marker for the healthy state of the relationship between sponsors and players. Rob also shared with the players several television advertisements that flighted in South Africa when the players were on tour. The players had never seen them before and the commercials were very emotive and very South African in how they spoke to rugby, sunny skies, braaing and having a Castle. The players loved watching the ads and it was one of those sessions that gave birth to the idea of featuring players in the commercials.

As I keep on saying, we have come a long way in 20 years and so much of what made 2019 spectacular had its roots in 2001. It wouldn't have been possible had Rian, as head of rugby in South Africa, not created the working portfolios within SA Rugby and the Springboks to add such value to the playing experience of being a Springbok.

Results do determine so much of a player's experience or any sponsorship alignment and partnership, and in those dark years when the Springboks slumped to seventh in the world, the player and sponsor may not always have felt a similar goodwill. But for me the good far outweighed even the worst of those years, and the sponsors would always come through for the team in various ways, with the belief that the Springboks would be good enough to play themselves back to the top of the rankings.

Sponsorships over the years became bigger, the investment became more and with it the demands on the players. There has been a huge evolution in how sponsorships work over the past 20 years, and there is a lot of detail in the contracts that differentiate tournament sponsors, series sponsors, team sponsors, kit sponsors, associate sponsors and broadcast sponsors from each other. In South Africa, SuperSport have been the exclusive broadcast sponsor for the past two decades and they've walked every mile with the Springboks, and walked many extra miles on behalf of a struggling Springbok performance or season.

Imtiaz Patel, who for much of that time drove the partnership from within SuperSport, played a massive role in South African rugby's transition from an amateur to professional sport and Rian and current SA Rugby CEO Jurie Roux always felt they had a professional ally at the table in Imtiaz. And by 'ally', I mean a world sports broadcast leader who also understood the dynamics of South African sport and in particular Springbok rugby. And for my part I had great support in working with SuperSport CEO Marc Jury and Thato Monale, the rugby executive producer.

The public couldn't be expected to be aware of how much alignment there is behind the scenes to ensure they get the best viewer experience and the most comprehensive coverage, but there is something very unique and South African about the relationship between the broadcaster and the national team. The people who work for SuperSport really do care about the Springboks and the players have come to understand the power of broadcast media and the strength of the many campaigns done with the Springboks. South Africans are very emotional and rugby is extremely emotive and all the most powerful advertising campaigns speak to this emotion and patriotism.

The Plettenberg Bay Springbok camp experience in 2001 was where I cut my teeth in team relationships with sponsors and partners. It was where I got my first insight into the adulation that there is for the Springboks, but also the cruelty that there can be from the South African rugby public in how they can verbally attack a player, based on their belief the player had underperformed.

Everyone will tell you it is part of the job, but I've never believed rudeness, crassness and insulting behaviour can in any way be justified, like on the evening we had lost to France in Johannesburg and supposed supporters, wearing Springbok jerseys, were urinating on the team bus outside the stadium. That incident in 2001 shocked me and thinking about it still shocks me. No one deserves that, least of all players who are giving their all to represent the country and win.

I have never met a Springbok player who deliberately lost in front of 60 000 people at the ground and wanted to play poorly knowing millions were watching on television, and I have never known a Springbok player to not care about the result or his performance. There were times I guess the team played poorly and others when the opposition was just too good, but you only had to be in the change room after a defeat to know how much it hurt the players. Some showed the hurt more than others, but I know every player felt the hurt and the management were as emotionally invested in the performance.

In my years with the Springboks, I would work under seven coaches, and they all had strengths and weaknesses and different personalities, but they all cared deeply about the result and took it personally when the Springboks lost. Some handled it better than others and different personalities made for differing perceptions, while some got more favourable press than others.

Harry, being the first Bok coach who I had experienced professionally, was also the most unique from a business point of view, but in hindsight perhaps his rugby language should have been more geared towards the simplicity of young men who knew how to play rugby very well, as opposed to a belief that he was addressing young business executives.

Harry had motivated to Rian why he felt the Springboks should have a separate business location away from SA Rugby's offices, and part of his reasoning was the need for privacy when it came to player interviews, player visits and selection meetings. The Springbok Business Unit lasted only as long as Harry did as coach, which was just 15 months.

I have very fond memories of 2001 because I got to experience the full spectrum of a Springbok cycle in the course of a few months, which included my first Tri-Nations, in which we lost to the All Blacks at Newlands, beat the Wallabies in Pretoria and drew with them in Perth, before losing to the All Blacks at Eden Park in Auckland.

That Tri-Nations had everything, from hope to despair, from believing to being buried, from experiencing a Test win at Loftus to my first experience of South African businessman David Rodwell and his wife Rita's hospitality towards the team in Perth, to the many South Africans living in Perth who still love the Springboks and, of course, the many South Africans living in Auckland who became South African for at least one day in the week that we were there. I also got to experience that painful and draining experience of being a South African at Eden Park when the All Blacks slowly suffocate the life out of a Springbok challenge.

My first year with the Springboks in 2001 had it all and within 24 hours of the first home Test I was finding out about the pressure that comes with a week in which there was no way the Boks could afford to lose a second successive Test (and consequently the series) against France. We lost that first Test in Johannesburg but went on to win in Durban one week later in a match that kept me very busy with all the drama of yellow cards, citings and disciplinary hearings.

I very quickly got to observe the intense pressure under which a Springbok coach operates, the pressure that gets extended to the captain and players and how unrelenting the media can be and how unforgiving the public can be when it comes to the Springboks.

The South African rugby public back then didn't take kindly to any defeat, especially if it was at home.

We won that second Test in Durban in 2001, but I will never forget how despondent Harry was at the team hotel. The Test was won on sheer physicality and it was a brutal contest, but Harry said it had felt to him like a defeat because of the kind of rugby the Springboks had played.

The players weren't down and they were just relieved that they'd won and could actually face the South African rugby public on the Saturday night and the following week. It was the type of situation that never really changed in that year with Harry, who perhaps realised he had arrived in a Springbok change room with a philosophy that would take 10 more years to reach the players in a sport that had only been professional for five years.

André Vos was the first Springbok captain I worked with and we remain friends today. He is such a well-rounded individual and such a gentleman. 'Vossie' was liked by every player and this was rare in the early 2000s when provincialism was very strong in the Springbok squad. His popularity is more impressive when you consider that Vossie, who played for the

Johannesburg-based Lions and Cats, captained a Bok team in the first two Tests against France that included Joost van der Westhuizen (Bulls), Corné Krige, Bob Skinstad (both Stormers) and Rassie Erasmus (Cats), vocal leaders who had captained their respective Super 12 teams.

The provincialism that was strong in 2001 never encroached on my thinking or interfered in the way I did my job because the players all interacted with me as Springboks and performed their responsibilities as such. The unified bond of national unity that was so prevalent in the 2007 World Cup win was one that had been developed under Jake and John in 2004 and every year it became stronger, with it being as strong as I have ever known it to be in 2019.

Back in 2001, in Port Elizabeth, the Springboks were playing Italy and Harry made the decision to drop Vossie as his captain and appoint Bob. It was a controversial decision, especially among the rugby media from up north who were not shy to express their dislike for the Stormers players and Bob, in particular. It also wasn't the ideal way to start the week's preparation.

The public relations fallout had the potential to be very damaging to the squad and I felt I owed it to Harry to let him know how I felt. I was confident that I could voice my opinion, but very naive in how I did it and what I actually said. I had quickly become a selector in my own mind and I told him that I thought he was wrong in replacing Vossie, why I thought he should stay captain and what I thought of Vossie as a rugby player. Harry very quickly let me know I did the public relations and he picked the team and that he would worry about the selection and I needed to worry about my portfolio.

It was the only time I ever had to be reprimanded for being a selector with Springbok coaches because I never again made that mistake. For the rest of my tenure I'd keep my rugby opinion to myself, especially when it came to the selection of the Test team and the captain. As a supporter, we are all selectors from our couch but that's very different from actually picking the team.

I love rugby and over the 20 years I've picked up a few things – I can recognise a training-ground move when it happens in a Test match, and I am familiar with the coaching language – but my job involved taking care of the well-being of those who played the rugby rather than the on-field rugby.

Harry put me firmly in my place and I will forever be grateful to him because he wasn't rude when he did it. He was very real in educating me about staying in my lane.

I will also forever be grateful to Harry for asking me to arrange an audience with the late President Mandela and the Springbok squad. Harry told me that it was very important to him that the players and management got to meet Mr Mandela and understand what he had fought for to make South Africa a democracy and an accepted part of the world.

Harry was an admirer of Mr Mandela, and the symbolism of Mr Mandela and the 1995 Springboks was never lost on Harry, who spoke to the players about the influence of 'Madiba' on the Springboks winning the 1995 World Cup and changing South Africa.

Harry was also the type of personality who didn't ask you if it was possible, but assumed that you would tell him when it was possible. I had never met Mr Mandela and I had never requested a team meeting with him, but it was assumed from Harry that it was a given that the team would be meeting with Mr Mandela and Bok assistant coach Tim Lane had even asked me if he could take along a copy of Mr Mandela's autobiography, *Long Walk to Freedom*, to be signed.

I now had a challenge to make it happen and I was given the name and number of Zelda la Grange, who was Mr Mandela's private secretary. My phone call to Zelda would not only lead Harry and the squad to Mr Mandela's Houghton residence, but it would also be a call that led to a lifetime friendship with Zelda and one that has given me access to the greatest sounding board for the past two decades.

Zelda was the gatekeeper to the world's most influential and in-demand person of our lifetime and it was something that kept me grounded whenever I felt overwhelmed at being the gatekeeper to the Springboks.

All it took was one phone call to Zelda to get perspective because if I thought I had it tough at times with the Springboks, it just did not compare to the pressures of Zelda's job.

Fourie du Preez – Bok captain

I was very fortunate to be involved with the Springboks for 12 years and, except for her brief stint with World Rugby, Annelee was there with us from the beginning to the end.

My favourite sight of her was always on game day. First, she was sorting out the wives and kids. Then helping with whatever issue there was with tickets. And finally, when getting to her seat at the stadium, she'd have this secret little whisky flask tucked away in her jacket to try settle her nerves.

After every Test, Annelee would show me how much was left and I knew that, if it was a very tight Test match, there would be nothing left!

Annelee, thank you for everything you did for us. And thank you for the memories.

Chapter 9

IT DOESN'T GET BIGGER THAN MEETING MADIBA

Typically, my schedule in the week of a Test match would run as follows: Sunday would be a travel day, so on my list would be to check the hotel bills, ensure that the luggage has gone, make sure everyone has been checked in at the airport and, if travelling to another country, there are no issues with visas and passports.

Everything is done to make it as easy as possible for the player, so that his only focus is rugby. I was part of the management group that would travel ahead of the players and attend to all the operational aspects, so for the player it was a matter of passing through security, customs (if going overseas) and settling in the business class lounge.

The operational group would book the players into the hotel and Sunday evening would consist of an operations team meeting, where all sponsor and media obligations would be confirmed and the weekly schedule would be shared with everyone. If there were commercial obligations, aligned with a Test, tour or tournament, then the details would be factored into the week and there was also usually a session, during the players' off-time, that involved jersey signings and Springbok memorabilia signings which, over the years, were reduced dramatically to preserve the value of these signed Springbok items, especially Test jerseys. The signing sessions are very controlled and they would start at 3pm and end at 4pm and there would be an inventory of how many jerseys needed to be signed.

My Monday would also involve getting in touch with a restaurant to arrange the team dinner, which was either on a Tuesday, Wednesday or Thursday, depending on who the coach was. I would visit the restaurant to ensure the menu met the diet and nutrition requirements or that it allowed for meals as agreed upon by the team dietician and conditioning coach, and I would make sure that the restaurant could accommodate the players in a way that the public intrusion was minimal and that they got privacy. I would always take the bus driver with me so that there were no issues with the route or the time it took to get to the restaurant and back to the hotel.

Monday, Tuesday and Wednesday were the big training days and I would accompany the forward group of the management to co-ordinate any on-field signing sessions and help JJ Fredericks and Charles Wessels set up whatever else may be necessary for the session.

My week was always spent in constant contact with sponsors because there was usually some form of player obligations for an advertisement, a photo shoot or a corporate commitment. I would try and schedule as many as possible in the mornings of the players' day off to minimise the disruption into the afternoon. Most of our bigger shoots and commercial gigs were done in the build-up to the international season, but it was rare that we would have a Test match week without doing something commercially related.

The Monday morning would also involve the preparation of the ticket list and if players knew they were playing it would determine the purchase of additional tickets. There was a combination of complimentary and bought tickets and I would arrange the pick-up and delivery and also be responsible for the sponsor ticket allocation and the VIP tickets.

The players would also request flights for their partners or wives and I'd work closely with each partner, wife or family member to confirm the flights and the accommodation when they were booked to stay at the team hotel. What only took a paragraph to write required several hours of planning early in the week to coordinate every player's family and extended family travel requests.

Over the years, the veterans among the players and management were so well versed in the procedure that they would sort their own family travel arrangements, but in any squad, some players, especially the younger and newer members, were more reliant on me doing it, and I knew that it meant there was one less thing for them to worry about.

Thursday afternoon was usually the players' downtime and I tried to limit them from having to do anything official or team related on the one afternoon they didn't have to think about rugby.

Friday morning involved the jersey presentation and team photo, a visit to the venue for their captain's run, which was more a walk-through for the players and a chance for everyone to familiarise themselves with the stadium and also for us to dress up the change room if we knew it wouldn't be practical to do it on match day. Charles, our head of operations, would replicate his minute-by-minute match-day travel schedule while I'd also confirm the team bus to ferry the wives, partners and children, and whatever was needed for them on arrival at the team hotel.

It was all very functional and structured but it made for an efficient and well-oiled machine and it all became second nature – the more I did it, year after year, the more my mind seemed to operate on autopilot.

But all of what went into a week's work in that first year, in terms of thought and stress levels, didn't match what I felt the first time I had to take the squad to meet with President Mandela at his Houghton residence in 2001. This was new territory for me and, through a series of calls to Mr Mandela's private secretary, Zelda la Grange, it had been arranged that Mr Mandela would see the players and management.

Zelda, who I had yet to meet in person, was charming and accommodating in our telephonic interactions. She explained the protocols around the dos and don'ts of the visit (the latter I can't recall) and she said Mr Mandela was looking forward to hosting 'his favourite boys'. I say I don't remember the don'ts because it seemed like nothing was off limits in the way Mr Mandela interacted with the players whenever they were in his company.

Mr Mandela wearing the Springbok No 6 jersey and handing the World Cup to Francois Pienaar after South Africa won the 1995 final against the All Blacks is probably the most famous rugby photo in the world, and so much had been written and broadcast about Madiba's love for rugby and the Springboks.

Harry Viljoen had been insistent that the squad must experience the magic of Mr Mandela and this was the first big adventure I had been asked to organise. It never got bigger than these visits to Mr Mandela, and every time I arranged with Zelda for a squad of players to meet him, it felt like I was experiencing it for the first time.

Zelda met me on the team's first arrival and when I got off the bus she was there to say hello and gave me this warm hug. It immediately calmed my nerves and she was just so polished, professional and in charge of the moment and situation. It was an education, professionally, to watch her work and to witness how she managed Mr Mandela's time during our visit. She knew just when to move it along, when not to interrupt a story or an interaction and she created an atmosphere that was so relaxed, which allowed the players and management to also relax.

Madiba's presence was awe-inspiring and this feeling never dulled, no matter how many times I found myself alongside Zelda and in his company. One particularly memorable time was when Jake White and I were invited to join them for lunch in Mr Mandela's kitchen at his Cape Town residence. They both made it feel like your standard lunch at home, but it wasn't because of who was sitting opposite us at the table.

It was the same at that very first visit in 2001, and Mr Mandela asked a lot of questions of the players, took an interest in all of them, and spoke about the power of sport as a unifier and also the power of the Springboks as ambassadors in South Africa and to the rest of the world. He posed for photos with each of the players and management, and gladly signed Tim Lane's copy of *Long Walk to Freedom*.

Within a minute of arriving, there was an overwhelming sense that we were in the presence of someone who was out of the ordinary, and every one of the squad members had a story to tell of the visit when we got back to the hotel.

Zelda and I had an instant connection, and she was so willing to speak about her experience as the private secretary to Mr Mandela and answer questions I had in relation to being this gatekeeper to the Springboks. She had so much insight into how to manage the public expectation and the demands that there would be on the players and coach, just by her experience of managing Mr Mandela's schedule.

I still marvel at what she did, how she did her job and with the balance she always showed in managing the engagements we, as the Springboks, had with Mr Mandela.

Zelda went out of her way to accommodate meetings between the squad and Mr Mandela. One of my fondest memories was when the team went to see him while he was on a visit to Paris during the early stages of the 2007 World Cup in France. Zelda had called me and said Mr Mandela wanted to see the boys and we quickly slotted into whatever time was available, and it proved to be another of those wonderful experiences. He told Jake and John to win the World Cup, bring it back to South Africa and to come visit him at his home with the trophy.

Jake and John had been part of a very significant photo shoot with Mr Mandela at his residence in Houghton in 2006. Mark Keohane, who had been with the Springboks as communications manager between 2000 and 2003, was working for *SA Rugby* magazine and he called me to see if a photo shoot with Mr Mandela could be arranged to celebrate the 100-year centenary of the Springboks.

I said I would try, but that I could promise nothing and that I would be guided by Zelda on what was possible. True of Zelda she made it happen and Mr Mandela was photographed in a Springbok blazer, especially designed for him, alongside the Springbok coach Jake White and captain John Smit.

Madiba had never before been photographed in a Bok blazer and it didn't happen again. He put on the blazer, did the shoot, Zelda removed the blazer and it was sent straight to the Nelson Mandela Museum.

Mark, who was writing the magazine's cover story, myself and the photographer, Lee Warren, were the only ones allowed at the photo shoot and Zelda gave us 30 minutes. It turned into a generous hour or more after the shoot when Mark and I got to spend some time alone chatting with Mr Mandela, whose presence was as powerful as it had been the first time I had met him. His laugh was infectious and his opening question in those meetings between 2004 and 2009 was always: 'Where is Os?' in reference to Springbok prop Os du Randt, who had won the World Cup in 1995 and come out of retirement to win it in 2007. Mr Mandela loved Os and while he also always spoke with such fondness of the 1995 Springbok World Cup-winning captain Francois Pienaar, in my time there wasn't a Springbok more popular with him than Os.

He was also very fond of Breyton Paulse and Chester Williams, and Joost van der Westhuizen was another who always got a mention whenever we visited, whether Joost was in the squad or not.

There wasn't one Madiba moment that was any less memorable than the other, but former Wallabies captain George Gregan will confirm the moment in 2005 when he knew they were in for tough afternoon at Ellis Park after his players bumped into the Springboks in the tunnel where Madiba was chatting to them before the game. George saw how awestruck his teammates were and realised it would take great mental resolve to beat the Springboks at Ellis Park with Nelson Mandela at the match. South Africa won 33-20.

I loved watching the players around Madiba; they hung on his every word and were like little kids visiting their favourite grandpa. The Springboks are forever indebted to Zelda for making it happen, even in those times when it seemed impossible given the demands on his schedule.

One of my favourite visits to Mr Mandela was when Jake, John and the squad were true to their promise and visited him upon their return from France after winning the 2007 World Cup, and Jake famously presented the trophy with the words: 'Mr Mandela, we promised you we'd bring home the cup, and here it is.'

Juan Smith – Bok captain

It is an absolute honour and privilege to pay tribute to Annelee Murray.

When I met Annelee for the first time, I knew she was special – a dynamic, trustworthy, passionate, strong woman. I wasn't wrong and she never disappointed.

Those were all the characteristics a person in Annelee's position had to have but it was never an easy task. Above and beyond looking after the players and management, the wives and children were also her responsibility.

She did her job with energy and passion. She was always open and willing to tackle tough situations head on and she found solutions for us, instead of going to management.

The void was felt by everyone when Annelee left the Springbok group for a while to work for World Rugby.

Annelee, it was a privilege to work with you for more than a decade in the Bok group. Thank you for your positive contribution.

We know it was not always an easy task. As the saying goes, 'A smooth sea never made a skilled sailor'. Annelee, you are indeed a skilled sailor!

Chapter 10

THE GOOD – THE ULTIMATE CHALLENGE

We had played the All Blacks a lot from 2001 to 2019 but I actually had to go and look it up to know just how many times I was fortunate to be a part of this great rugby rivalry. During that period, we played each other 43 times – 20 matches in New Zealand, 20 in South Africa and three at neutral venues during the 2003 World Cup in Australia (Melbourne), the 2015 World Cup in England (Twickenham, London) and the 2019 World Cup in Japan (Yokohama). We won 10 of those Tests, one was drawn and the All Blacks won 32. Each one of those 10 Test wins and the draw in Wellington in 2019 are moments I have banked for the rest of my life. To put it into perspective, in the history of the game England have beaten the All Blacks just eight times, and they weren't trekking down to New Zealand every year to play them.

There isn't a bigger challenge in the game for the Springboks than going to New Zealand to play the All Blacks and there isn't a bigger moment on the Test calendar than going to New Zealand and being part of a team that beats the All Blacks. When I reflect on the Tests that I have been involved in over 20 years, it is those winning moments against the All Blacks that take pride of place.

I am not including the two World Cup final wins in 2007 and 2019, or the 2009 series victory against the British & Irish Lions, as those obviously are career highlights. But if you speak to the Springbok players and management, they will tell you just how much it means to them to beat the All Blacks in New Zealand.

I cherish every one of those change-room moments in New Zealand when we came out tops. The one that will always be that little bit more special is the last-minute win at Carisbrook in Dunedin in 2008. The Springboks had never won in Dunedin, and the old Carisbrook – where Otago and the

Highlanders used to play their provincial and Super Rugby matches – was called the House of Pain. I'd experienced my fair share of pain with the Springboks in New Zealand since my first Bok experience at Eden Park in Auckland in 2001, and no matter how many times I toured New Zealand, it never got any easier and the rugby experience never got any less tense.

There is no other international rugby experience like going to New Zealand because not only are the All Blacks the hardest team to beat in the world, but their public are fanatical in supporting them, and their supporters' passion for the Test match occasion can be suffocating for any opposition team. I always found the Springboks to be a very popular team with the New Zealand media and public. Our training sessions were always well attended and the Kiwis always made a big fuss about having the Springboks in town. My working week in New Zealand was hectic with PR, media requests and fan requests, and there was a big demand for the Springboks to have at least one training session open to the public. Many of those who attended were South Africans who had moved to New Zealand.

I always got the sense that the New Zealand media and public wanted us to be competitive and do well, if not necessarily to ever beat the All Blacks. But on those occasions when we did, their media were complimentary and their public acknowledged the quality of the win and the class of our players, many of whom had become household names in New Zealand through Super Rugby performances and the annual Tri-Nations or Rugby Championship Tests against the All Blacks.

Throughout my years of travelling to New Zealand with the Springboks, the intensity of the week building up to the Test match was always at a peak. Whether we were in form and being written up or struggling and not given much hope, there was always this acknowledgement of the rugby history between the two teams and daily reminders of the rivalry and the great Test matches. For the players, it was the match they wanted to play in, even if the week of the Test was always the toughest mental challenge. Wherever you went you were reminded you were playing the All Blacks and everyone had an opinion on the match, the Springboks and the players.

I remember being in Christchurch one year and having a coffee with Danie Rossouw and some of the other players who had won Super Rugby with the Bulls. The woman who served us reminded Danie of something he had done playing for the Bulls that season and she felt he could have done it better because she said he was that good a player. I was blown away by the detail and rugby technicality of her conversation. I think Danie was as shocked as I was.

That kind of thing happened often and while the players enjoyed New Zealand's scenic beauty and the familiarity of having travelled there every year for Super Rugby, it did not relieve the pressure of a Test match week.

Lisa Kingi-Bon, my good friend who had worked at SA Rugby before moving to New Zealand to work for the New Zealand Rugby Union, would tell me that the Springboks, at times, seemed to respect the All Blacks players too much. She wasn't being critical of us, but she felt that we had always put them on too high a pedestal and that they were just as normal and vulnerable as our guys. She had worked for both unions and had an insight into both teams and felt that if we humanised them a bit more, we'd beat them more often.

I enjoyed visiting New Zealand and I have made many good friends there in the past 20 years, but there was nothing quite as satisfying as being a part of a Springbok win in New Zealand. In two decades of travelling the world, we'd played in 47 cities in 12 countries but the two nights that remain big for me were the 2008 and 2009 wins in Dunedin and Hamilton in New Zealand. It was unheard of to beat the All Blacks in successive Tests, but we did it, and in 2009 we would win three Tests in a row against the All Blacks, with two of them being in South Africa.

When I look back on 20 years of Springbok Test matches, I remember the good, the bad and the ugly, and I have narrowed it down to my 10 best Test match experiences, based on results, the occasion and just being in that change room. As you may have guessed, every one of the three wins and one draw in New Zealand make the top 10. There are also a few wins against the All Blacks in South Africa that feature and one very big day at Twickenham.

That night in Dunedin in 2008 was magical, even though the build-up had been difficult because we had lost the previous week in Wellington, and this was the first Test match between the All Blacks and Springboks since we had won the World Cup in France in 2007. When we got to New Zealand the media questioned whether our players felt they could call themselves world champions because they had not beaten the All Blacks at the World Cup. I remember John joking that it wasn't our doing that we hadn't played New Zealand, and that we had held up our end of the agreement, which was to get to Paris for the evening of the final on the 20th

October. It was a great response from John, who was very comfortable and confident when interacting with the media.

The question repeatedly put to the players in that week was whether they felt worthy of being world champions and our players were consistent in that they most certainly felt worthy, given they had beaten every team they faced at the World Cup. New Zealand had lost to France in the quarter-final of the 2007 World Cup and they were eager to avenge the early exit by beating the world champion Springboks in Wellington.

As always, we knew how tough the match would be, but there was a belief in the squad that we were good enough to beat the All Blacks, and Peter de Villiers, who had succeeded Jake White as coach, had appointed Gary Gold and Dick Muir as his assistant coaches and retained John as his captain.

Peter had lots of energy and a very positive outlook which complemented the personalities of Gary and Dick and the senior player group of John, Victor Matfield, Fourie du Preez, Bryan Habana and Percy Montgomery. I had been part of preparations for Test matches in New Zealand under Harry Viljoen (2001), Rudolf Straeuli (2002) and Jake White (2004-2007), but Peter's demeanour encouraged the players to be relaxed and to focus on the enjoyment of being able to play rugby for their country. He also allowed each member of the management to get on with their job and he never interfered in my portfolio. We really had a good vibe as a squad in New Zealand in 2008 and a lot of fun was had off the field. Peter wanted the players and management to live the experience of touring and of being Springboks and not become obsessed with exclusively focusing on just the Test match day, and he preached that a happy team was a successful team.

We had a lot of hope going into the Test match but we lost John to a groin injury after All Blacks lock Brad Thorn spear tackled him. Australian Stuart Dickinson was the referee and he only penalised Brad, who was later cited by the match commissioner and suspended for the next Test in Dunedin.

Brad, to his credit, sought out John straight after the game and apologised for the tackle and said there was no excuse. John accepted Brad's handshake and said there was no ill-feeling, although the coaches were angry that the tackle had ended his match and his tour. John retained his sense of humour at what he called 'another bloody defeat in New Zealand' and he was on the plane home to South Africa the next day.

I was devastated for John because I knew how desperate he was to win a Test in New Zealand and he felt that we had such a good chance of not only winning one but both Tests in 2008. We lost 19-8 in Wellington and John was gone, but Peter, Dick and Gary insisted that we were very close in Wellington and that if lady luck stuck around in Dunedin, and we played to our ability, we would win. They said it was time for the world champions to make some history and be the first Springbok team to win in Dunedin, and what better venue, given that it was where the All Blacks had played the Springboks for the first time ever.

Dunedin is very different to Wellington, which is similar to Cape Town and has a vibrant city feel to it. Dunedin is renowned for being a student town and if ever you felt trapped on tour in New Zealand, and with no escape, it was for the 24 hours in Dunedin before the Test or those 12 hours after the Test if we had lost. Queenstown, not far from Dunedin, is the adventure capital of the world and just absolutely stunning, and often the Bok players, when we were scheduled to play in Dunedin, would be thrilled to be spending the week preparing in Queenstown.

In 2008, Peter's first year as coach, there was an innocence about the pressure of the job that fuelled a freedom in the attitude of the players, and the 2008 and 2009 trips to New Zealand rank as my most enjoyable and happiest. To me, the four-year cycle with Peter, Dick and Gary were some of my happiest management times and among the most relaxed and enjoyable.

In the build-up to the night we won at the House of Pain in Dunedin, John had sent the squad a good luck message from the plane back home to start his rehab. He admitted to being jealous of those who would be playing because he said he had a feeling that the night was going to belong to the Springboks. He told the squad he was convinced they were going to win – a message that corresponded with what the squad had been getting all week from the coaches. The players and all of us in the management fed off this positivity.

The New Zealand media picked up on this attitude within the squad and they spoke and wrote of a Bok backlash based on the world champions not wanting to leave New Zealand with two successive defeats. Some players read the media and some don't but, in Dunedin that week, what mattered much more than what was being written in the media was what was being said in every team meeting. The message was that it was going to be a history-making night for South African rugby.

Every such night has a hero and that hero normally is an unlikely one, and so it proved in Dunedin when Ricky Januarie scored the most spectacular solo try in the 75th minute and Frans Steyn kicked the conversion for us to win 30-28.

I don't know how I didn't suffer heart failure in those last few minutes as I paced up and down at Carisbrook, edging towards the field when it looked like we could win and then taking flight when it looked like it was all going wrong again. It was such a frantic match and my whisky flask had been used. I watched, then didn't and then watched again. And just when I thought it was ours to win, Victor Matfield, who was captaining the team, got yellow-carded. It seemed so wrong but so typical of our luck in New Zealand. You feel everything has gone right and then it goes wrong and, in that moment, I thought we had lost again, only for Ricky to go rogue on the All Blacks and score one of the most famous tries in our rugby history.

I couldn't contain myself. I jumped for joy, landed on the slippery surface near the field and fell into the mud with a field-side security man witnessing my leap and landing, and very generously offering me his hand to get up again. As I did, he said 'well done … you guys deserved it.' Little did I know then but I would hear those exact words from All Blacks coach Steve Hansen the night after the Springboks won the World Cup in 2019.

Carisbrook was an old-school rugby stadium and the change rooms made today's best Test match venue change rooms seem like luxury apartments. But on that night, everything was big enough, warm enough and good enough in that old change room. I remember looking at Percy Montgomery, who had just played his 99th Test for the Springboks, and he was just beaming.

Monty was the only player in the match-day squad who had known the feeling of beating the All Blacks in New Zealand, back at the old Athletic Park in Wellington in 1998. He told the squad that it was 'bullshit' that he had to wait 10 years between wins, and later that night, or it could have been in the early hours of the morning, he challenged the players to go one better and come back to New Zealand in 2009 and win again. And as he said it, everyone believed it would happen.

Dunedin, in 2008, was a D-Day moment for me in the Springbok group because it made every year of heartache in New Zealand worthwhile. Having finally experienced that winning feeling, the team just wanted more, and in 2009 the very same players who had made history in Dunedin would continue to write their own history against the All Blacks and the British & Irish Lions.

Gary Botha – Bok captain

When I was called up to the Springbok squad I noticed this friendly and very organised lady by the name of Annelee Murray – a woman who was behind the scenes, friendly, hardworking and always treated everyone with the same amount of respect.

There are so many stories that can be told about this lady and what she meant to and did for the Bokke. Annelee created order behind the scenes and linked the players, the management and everything else you can think of.

I was privileged to be a midweek Bok captain with Chiliboy Ralapelle in Leicester, England, when the Springboks played a World XV team. Pressure was high as always when you represent your country, but Annelee had this way of taking it away from a player due to her organising everything, and we could just pitch up and play.

The amount of effort that she went through to prepare team excursions and dinners was amazing.

You could approach her for help with anything and, without this lady, nothing would have been the same for the Springboks.

Thank you, Annelee, for the service that you have given our country and being a true custodian of Springbok rugby.

Chapter 11

THE GOOD – SETTING THE STANDARD

Peter de Villiers consulted with his coaches and decided to keep the Springboks in Brisbane in Australia to prepare for the 2009 Tri-Nations decider against the All Blacks in Hamilton, New Zealand.

The players loved being in Brisbane because of the weather and while the defeat to the Wallabies had come as a surprise, the players knew that victory in Hamilton would win the Tri-Nations. Once again we found ourselves in a situation with everything to play for, but against our biggest rivals and in New Zealand's backyard.

It was a good call to prepare in the relative rugby union obscurity of Brisbane and the Gold Coast, which meant that the players could switch on mentally for the rugby but also switch off from any distractions, which wouldn't have been possible if we had immediately travelled to Hamilton.

The decision to stay in Brisbane was popular with the players and management, but it wasn't very popular with the New Zealand media, and Peter's comment that 'there was nothing to do in Hamilton in any case' only added to the frosty reception that greeted us when we arrived in Auckland on the Thursday evening and then took a bus straight to Hamilton. It was about a two-hour drive, made less arduous for us because I had arranged a treat with Nando's New Zealand. They met us at the airport bus, and there was so much excitement when the players received these wonderful Nando's hampers – there wasn't much talking on that bus ride to Hamilton.

The fact that the Springboks had beaten the All Blacks twice in South Africa must have been the reason we could sense there was a lot trepidation in the media and a notable absence of the usual bravado.

We had prepared very well in Brisbane and there was so much conviction among the players in the possibility of winning. John would often talk about 'conviction and hope' and that there was a difference in attitude when it came to players and their preparation. If there was hope, it meant there wasn't always the belief within the squad, but when there was that conviction in attitude and talk, then the expectation of victory had been created by the players themselves, and that was when he felt the most confident that the talk would be backed up with a victorious performance.

John had won in New Zealand with the Sharks in Super Rugby but he had never won in New Zealand against the All Blacks as he had missed the historic 2008 win in Dunedin because of injury. Now, one year later, he was back in New Zealand, captaining a Springbok team playing for the Tri-Nations title and one that had twice beaten the All Blacks in South Africa.

There was no doubt that the players knew they were good enough to beat the All Blacks, but this was an All Blacks team determined to win after losing to us twice in a row, and they would have Dan Carter starting at No 10 after he had missed the two Tests in South Africa.

Personally, because of my friendship with John and the admiration that I had for him as the Springbok captain, this was the one win I desperately wanted. I knew he felt he had been so close in 2008, and beating the All Blacks in New Zealand was the one thing missing for him as a Springbok. Most of the players in Hamilton had won in Dunedin the year before, and it made for such a different mindset when we got to Hamilton. We would win in the most dramatic fashion by just three points (32-29). My nerves were gone again and so was the contents of my whisky flask, but the party that night among the squad was one of the biggest I have known because it was just the squad, at the team motel in Hamilton.

Our motel, on the outskirts of Hamilton, was 10 minutes at the most from the stadium. And on the way there we drove past a bemused Charles Wessels having a breathalyser test after our forward party, obviously part of the Springbok convoy, had been senselessly pulled over by the Hamilton Police Department. It was a moment the players enjoyed reminding Charles about for many years to come.

There weren't travelling fans so the night didn't have the off-field frenzy of a World Cup final with thousands of South African supporters close by. Poignantly, it was a celebration that took place within the squad and in the simplicity of four walls so far removed from the bright lights of the biggest cities in which we usually played our Tests.

I have so many photos of that night that make me smile every time I look at them. What a great night and early morning! What a feeling to beat the

All Blacks twice in a row in New Zealand and to quote Peter, in the early hours of the morning: 'I got it wrong, there is actually something to do in Hamilton ...'

One of John's character traits is that he doesn't take himself too seriously and he can laugh at himself and also recognise the need for a light moment when the situation appears hopeless, and losing to the All Blacks in New Zealand for him year after year was that kind of hopeless situation.

Former All Blacks captain Richie McCaw is one of the greatest to have played the game and such a gentleman and professional off the field, but if he had one rugby vulnerability early on in his rugby career, it was his public speaking. Richie was a great player and ambassador for the game and New Zealand rugby, but he never seemed comfortable having to make speeches at the post-match functions, whereas John, in full head boy mode, was a natural public speaker.

On the Friday night, I had joked with John: 'Wouldn't it be great if you lost the speaking contest for once, but won the game?' I said it with a laugh but deep down I meant it as a challenge because the thought of another winning speech from Richie, and a losing speech from John, was just unbearable.

Well, on this one and only time in a decade of playing Test rugby against the All Blacks in New Zealand when John was in the team or leading them, he and the guys came good. Yes, we won and I finally got to see him giving a winning speech and Richie in the very unfamiliar role of losing captain in New Zealand.

And, you guessed it, John nailed the speech. I couldn't stop smiling; I felt so proud and so happy for the team, and especially John. The one thing we all agreed on was that feeling of beating the All Blacks in New Zealand was one that we could all get used to, even though we knew it wasn't one we could ever take for granted.

Nobody said it out loud, but we could all get used to years like 2009, beating the All Blacks three times in succession and winning the British & Irish Lions series in South Africa, with the second Test against the Lions at Loftus Versfeld making the top 10 moments in my Test career. I have never experienced an atmosphere like I did that afternoon in Pretoria. It was a home Test but it felt like we were playing in the heart of the United Kingdom, with so many Lions supporters in the crowd. Loftus was a sea of red and I've not known a Test match in South Africa to ever replicate that kind of crowd noise and intensity.

Jaque Fourie scored an amazing try and Morné Steyn kicked the winning penalty with the last kick of the game, and we won the match (28-25) and the series. It was mayhem on the field and it got just as crazy and wild with the celebrations in the change room. To be in the Bok change room that evening was amazing and I knew I was a part of something special. Morné was central to everyone's happiness that night, just like he would be a few weeks later when the Springboks beat the All Blacks 31-19 in Durban and Morné set a record, scoring all 31 points.

I still marvel at that performance and Morné's humility afterwards. I've seen the odd player believe his own press and lose the plot in terms of significance and self-importance because of what they have done on the field, but I would say that Morné, Monty, Frans Steyn, André Pretorius and Handré Pollard were the quintessential expression of the Springbok ethos.

No matter how many points they scored and how many times they contributed to Springbok wins, they were the very same people who hadn't scored a point one minute before the kick-off.

The Springboks' win against the All Blacks in Durban was a particularly big moment for me professionally because not only did we beat them for a second Saturday in a row, but their coaches conceded they wanted to learn from us what made us successful and so difficult to beat.

When we were in New Zealand, Dick Muir was asked in a media interview what defined this Springbok team and he said 'happiness'. Dick told the New Zealand media that we all enjoyed each other's company. We all made each other smile and enjoyed doing things for each other. It may seem so simple but finding that harmony and enjoyment was key to our success.

Happiness, enjoyment and patriotism. The guys played for the people of South Africa, as much as they did themselves and their family. Singing the anthem was big for the players. Putting smiles on the faces of supporters was important and we know that South Africa is a happier country on a Monday when the Springboks have won. The jersey was important for the players, but the country was bigger than the jersey. The Springboks, in my tenure, have never just been a sporting team, but more an extension of a country that has had to come to terms with its past but is inspired by the possibilities of its future.

Richie was always generous in his praise for the Springboks, even when his teams were regularly beating us in New Zealand and South Africa, and he went on record to say that the 2009 Springboks were the best team he ever faced as an All Black. When you consider he played 148 Tests and lost just 15 of them, there can't be a bigger endorsement of the 2009 Springboks and there can't be bigger praise for the team that Jake and John had taken to the 2007 World Cup, and Peter and John had further evolved in 2008 and 2009.

In his autobiography, Richie wrote that All Blacks coaches Graham Henry, Wayne Smith and Steve Hansen were the first to make their way into our change room after the Springboks won in Durban because they wanted to experience what it was that made us so special.

What he wrote gave me goose bumps because it was a reflection of so much that I, as part of many different management teams, had worked so hard to achieve. Richie wrote that the feedback the coaches gave the All Blacks players was that they weren't playing against a team but against a nation. They spoke of how our change room looked, how it had been dressed up and decorated, how the country's flag and words of the anthem were displayed and how the change room spoke to the pride of a nation and not just a rugby team.

Richie wrote that the All Blacks coaches visiting the Springbok change room in 2009 was a defining moment in reshaping and changing attitudes within the All Blacks, where they had to look beyond the inspiration of the jersey and connect more with their supporters, and that it inspired so much of their patriotism and understanding of their responsibility towards their supporters at the 2011 World Cup in New Zealand.

Reading what he had written, many years after it had happened, was huge in the context of my Springbok career because while Morné had scored 31 points to win the game, there was a team of players and coaches behind him, and there was a management team behind that team. And behind that team there was a sponsorship and broadcast team, and behind all of that there was the most incredible fan base. The All Blacks coaches experienced this when they came to our change room to understand why they couldn't beat us in South Africa.

What a compliment from the All Blacks and what a compliment for all of South Africa and the impact of the country's emotional investment in the Springboks.

Chiliboy Ralepelle – Bok captain

A mother to everyone. That is what Annelee is to the Springboks – a caring, loving, encouraging woman behind the players.

Just like a mother, Annelee would leave all her personal needs behind so the players could find comfort and have everything they needed to be happy outside the game.

She was the one supporting and lifting our spirits whenever we felt down. Annelee is one of the kindest and warmest hearts I've experienced. She effortlessly spreads smiles and joy to everyone she meets. Through all our differences, her love was constant and she treated everyone equally.

As players, we always knew that our family was at ease in her presence. She made sure that our loved ones were taken care of before and after games.

I will be forever grateful to have spent my professional rugby career alongside this amazing woman.

Ke a leboga, Mme Annelee!

Chapter 12

THE GOOD – WITNESSING HISTORY

Every time the Springboks won was a good day for me, but there were those days that were extraordinarily good and, in my 20 years with the Springboks, they mostly involved matches against New Zealand and England. When I chat about the darkest and ugliest times in the change room, it is also predominantly after matches against England and New Zealand.

But that's for the next chapter; this one is still about those wonderful Test-winning experiences that extended beyond the 2007 and 2019 World Cup finals against England.

Not surprisingly, Emirates Airline Park (Ellis Park) played host to the most incredible night of my career in South Africa and a popular win against the All Blacks, but nothing in my Tests in South Africa matched the emotion of the night Siya Kolisi led the Springboks into battle in the first Test against England in 2018.

The build-up had been as intense as I'd known because Rassie Erasmus, in his first fortnight as the national coach, had to send a team to Washington DC to play Wales and keep one in South Africa to prepare for the first of two Tests against Eddie Jones' England.

The squad that went to the United States was captained by Pieter-Steph du Toit, but was very inexperienced and only a handful of those players, including Pieter-Steph, would be involved in the first Test against England. The public and media's focus seemed to be on England and not the one-off Test against Wales in DC, but Rassie's mind was firmly on both matches as he felt they were important in the building of depth for the 2019 World Cup in Japan.

Everything Rassie did was geared towards making – and winning – the World Cup final in Japan and the preparation of every Test over the 18 months leading into the World Cup was focused on winning in Japan.

Whatever we did as a management in the week of a Test in 2018 and 2019 had to speak to what we would be doing at the World Cup in Japan.

The trip to Washington DC was brutal. We flew economy class on Ethiopian Airlines via Johannesburg, Addis Ababa and Dublin. It took us 45 hours, we were in DC for 60 hours – including playing the Test match – and the travel back to Johannesburg was 47 hours. Rassie's culture was always one of no excuses, no whining and not feeling sorry for ourselves, but there were times in that week that I think everyone felt justified in feeling a bit flat.

South African golfer David Frost popped into visit the squad and there were South African supporters at the hotel who brought good energy, but it was so rushed in terms of a Test match week and it was very much a case of getting in, hopefully getting the job done, and then getting out and back to South Africa as quickly as possible.

The occasion wasn't particularly grand, it was played at the old RFK Stadium in DC and there wasn't much local hype around the match. Rassie had picked seven new caps for the Wales Test and we came within five minutes of winning it. We led 20-17 before a mistake led to Wales scoring and winning the Test 22-20.

Rassie was huge again in rallying the youngsters and while he never accepted defeat, he looked at what the individual victories were and what he could take from the trip that would benefit the Springboks in Japan in 2019. In those early weeks, the word 'depth' was something he spoke about so much and he kept on instilling it in the players that a team of 15 was never going to win the World Cup, it would take every squad member to make the Springboks world champions. His message extended to the management because everyone played a part and had to be at their best.

That trip back from DC was long and tiring, and for someone like Pieter-Steph to come back from that kind of week and still be a factor against England just tells you everything you need to know about his character. His dad, Pieter-Steph Senior, travelled to the US capital to watch his son captain the Boks and there was a mad dash to secure him a visa at the last minute.

The biggest talking point in the build-up to that first Test was Siya's appointment as captain and the history that would be made because he was the first black player to captain the Springboks in a Test match. Chiliboy Ralepelle had co-captained the Springboks against a World XV in Leicester in 2006, but it was not a Test match. Chiliboy was no stranger to captaincy, having captained the SA U21s at the World Championship in France, and he and Gary Botha, who also played hooker, were named co-captains for the match against the World XV with each playing one half. Chiliboy's appointment was a big moment in Springbok rugby, but Siya's 12 years later was even bigger because it was a Test match.

Siya leading the players onto the field on 9 June 2018 was a moment equally as special as 24 June 1995 when Nelson Mandela, dressed in a Springbok No 6 jersey, handed over the World Cup to Francois Pienaar. Both occasions took place at Emirates Airline Park, a stadium that had been known around the world since 1928 as Ellis Park.

Rassie didn't get caught up in the political significance of the moment and was consistent in his message that Siya had been selected because he was the best option. The coach never spoke about black, coloured or white in the team context, but he never shied away from talking about transformation and what was needed to transform the national team and the way the South African public perceived the Springboks.

I knew how the media would react to Siya's appointment and I'd been in the Bok system for long enough to know that black player numbers were always a media discussion before and after every Test team was named. I knew how big this week was and the team that Rassie had named to play England would have an impact on the reporting.

Jake White, in July 2005, had picked a Springbok team with six players of colour in the starting XV and eight in the match-day squad to play the Wallabies at Ellis Park for the Nelson Mandela Challenge Plate. Mr Mandela was among the 62 000 in attendance for the match and he had celebrated his 87th birthday in the week of the Test. John Smit and Jake had promised Mr Mandela a win as a 'birthday present' from the Bok coach and captain, and they were true to their word as we won 33-20.

When Siya stepped onto Ellis Park in 2018, I knew it was the biggest step for transformation in Springbok rugby and I was beyond excited.

The expectation was enormous in the week of the England Test because it felt like the entire country's eyes were on the Springboks, and it was the most inclusive and expanded media coverage of the Springboks that I had yet experienced. Every radio station, network and television broadcaster showed an interest in the Test match, and internationally the coverage was as extensive.

I had experienced the increase of those numbers among media interested in the Springboks, the changing dynamic of the Springboks over two

WAT

PREVIOUS PAGE: Lining up for the anthem with Tanu and assistant coach Johann van Graan.
ABOVE: Madiba's farewell speech to the Boks before the 2003 World Cup.
TOP RIGHT: Dr Yusuf Hassan on the team bus after the 2007 final.
RIGHT: JP, Wayne and Akona show off their medals.

ISSUE
RUGBY
2007

SPRINGBOK

ABOVE: Mac Hendricks and Flippie Molokoane in the Bok change room in 2006.
TOP RIGHT: Monty and Victor at a post-match function.
RIGHT: John and I at the Sydney Harbour Bridge in 2005.

ABOVE: With Odwa and Chiliboy at a team dinner in Sydney, 2010.
BELOW: Ernie Els presents the Bok jerseys in London, 2004.

ABOVE: Hanging out with Butch, Breyton and Jaque.
BELOW: At a fuction with Vossie (André Vos) and AJ.

ABOVE: Lunch with Madiba and Jake in Constantia, Cape Town, 2006.
BELOW: Monty and Bryan during the 2007 Trophy Tour.

ABOVE & BELOW: Giving the Bok change room our special touch.

ABOVE: Allister, Gert and Eddie with 'William' in 2007.
BELOW: Dick got a hole-in-one at St Andrews on a day off in 2010.

ABOVE: Daliah, Rene and I with the Freedom Cup and Tri-Nations trophy in Hamilton, 2009.
BELOW: With Vivian Verwant and Flippie in the Bok change room.

ABOVE: A bowling evening with the guys in Cardiff, 2008.
BELOW: Gio Aplon is capped in Cardiff, 2010.

ABOVE: With Gary at the Millennium Stadium in 2008.
BELOW: The end of Rassie's playing career coincided with the start of my time with the Boks.

ABOVE: The team meets Madiba in 2005.
BELOW: Madiba in the Bok change room at Loftus.

ABOVE: Monty was very chuffed to meet Madiba in 2002.
BELOW: Showing off our impressive trophy haul from 2004 on a beautiful Cape Town beach.

ABOVE: Celebrating our British & Irish Lions series win in 2009 with Bryan and a cigar.
BELOW: A team dinner with Peter and Gary in London, 2010.

ABOVE: The Boks' security detail at the 2007 World Cup.

BELOW: Johan, Albert and Johann wearing the Bok centenary jersey in Dublin, 2006.

DÔME
LEDGE
20
Zone

TOP LEFT: Daliah, Dick and Peter in Auckland, 2010.
BOTTOM LEFT: My friend Lisa Kingi-Bon and her husband Mahau in Hamilton, 2009.
ABOVE: Siya and his son Nic at the 2015 World Cup in England.

TOP: Visiting Madiba at his home in Houghton after the 2007 World Cup.
ABOVE: Fourie, wearing his 50th Test cap, with his wife Janét in Perth, 2009.
TOP RIGHT: With Joe Locke, the All Blacks media manager, at Liv Village, Durban.
BOTTOM RIGHT: Zelda supporting the Boks in Port Elizabeth, 2010.

ALL BLACKS
adidas
AIG
ALL BLACKS

ABOVE: Catching up with former Bok assistant coach Tim Lane in Brisbane, 2016.
TOP RIGHT: Sitting in the front row with Ruan and Bryan for a squad photo in 2014.
BOTTOM RIGHT: Management team members in the Bok change room, 2011.

ABSA
ABSA

TOP: Juan on the 2007 Trophy Tour.
ABOVE: Gary and Bok technical analyst Malome Maimane in 2010.
TOP RIGHT: Visiting Edinburgh Castle on an off-day in 2010.
BOTTOM RIGHT: Ernie Els braai at his home in Wentworth, England (2006).

sasol

ABOVE: A team lunch on Women's Day in Cape Town with Lukhanyo, Sikhumbuzo and Lwazi.
TOP RIGHT: Lunch at The Oval in London with Saracens players and George North.
BOTTOM RIGHT: Faf du Plessis and Russell Domingo with Bok coach and captain in 2016.

SURREY
THE KIA OVAL England v South Africa

BLUE LABEL
TELECOMS

ABOVE: A quick photo with Schalk at the Palazzo Hotel before a jersey presentation.
TOP RIGHT (clockwise from left): Heyneke, Eben, Beast and Adriaan at a jersey presentation in Nelspruit; team photo in Florence for my 200th Test in 2016.
RIGHT: In the tunnel at Twickenham.

ABSA

ABSA
ABSA
ABSA

WE AR
ANY
RE ONE
ABSA
ABSA

ABOVE: At a function with Allister.
TOP RIGHT: The Bok change room at Kings Park.
BOTTOM RIGHT: At the 2015 World Cup with Daliah.

SPRINGBOKS
SPRINGBOKS
SPRINGBOKS
SPRINGBO
INGBOKS

The Spirit of Rugby
#RWC 2015

ABOVE: Warming up with Rene and Tanu on a freezing Buenos Aires training day in 2016.

decades and the growth of players like Siya, from the shy young man who I had welcomed to the Test team in June 2013 and who made his Test debut one week later in a Man of the Match performance against Scotland at the Mbombela Stadium in Nelspruit.

The Siya of 2013 was as humble as the more mature and experienced player named to captain the Springboks against England in 2018. The captaincy announcement took Siya by surprise because Rassie casually confirmed it at a team meeting. There was no fanfare or fuss from Rassie in naming Siya captain – after confirming the match-day squad to the players, he added that Siya would be captain for the England series and there was a round of applause for Siya, who looked shocked at the announcement.

Rassie, in the two years I worked alongside him in 2018 and 2019, was the master of understated moments, and the naming of Siya as captain was one of the most powerful.

The coach did not get caught up with media talk of black player numbers, of players being ambassadors and role models and of the Springboks being symbolic of change in South Africa. He kept on telling the players that they had to earn the right to be respected, to be spoken about and to be seen as ambassadors to South Africa, and that the only way they could earn that right was to become a winning team and the best team in the world. Only then would people look up to them, be inspired by them and want to be like them.

I don't have to explain to you how active the public relations and media portfolios within the team were that week of the first Test against England, who had arrived in South Africa as one of the best sides in the world and one of the form teams since Eddie had been appointed coach in late 2015.

The week was like a World Cup final being hosted in South Africa and everything was about Siya's captaincy and the racial make-up of the squad because never before had a Springbok Test side included as many players of colour. But it was not a topic Rassie would engage in publicly and, when he was repeatedly asked about it, he would talk about the rugby and what he considered rugby decisions. He said he had picked a squad he felt could beat England and they would be judged on whether they could do this.

I had never known a Test crowd at Ellis Park to be so representative of South Africans and the atmosphere was unlike any other Bok Test match I'd experienced. It was one big rugby carnival in the stands and everything Siya had told the media he expected it to be in the Friday press conference.

'The people get behind you [at Ellis Park]. It is really special. They sing the whole anthem equally. You see the whole of South Africa, the different races and different colours. It is one of the most beautiful things I have seen. They get behind you and they always turn up,' was how Siya described Ellis Park as a Test occasion.

He also said that he wasn't focusing on the symbolism of wearing the Springbok No 6 jersey at Ellis Park, like Madiba famously had in the same month, 23 years earlier, and that all he could control was his own performance.

'I don't think of that. I am a calm guy. I have to make sure that I play well and if there is outside pressure then it may be too much for me,' he told the media. 'I have been relaxed. The coach has made it simple for me and I just have to perform. When I first captained the Stormers I took everything on myself, but here I have great leaders from other unions who will help.'

Siya had also lightened the mood by recalling his Test debut against Scotland and how Jean de Villiers, who was the Springbok captain, had proved such a calming influence.

'I remember everything about my Test debut,' he said. 'I was on the bench and I remember spitting water for no reason. I was really nervous and then within five minutes of the start I was told to warm up because there was an injury to Arno Botha. As I went on, Johann van Graan [the assistant coach] told me to forget about everything. I had trouble remembering things and he told me just to play my game.

I was sitting next to Siya's dad, Fezakele Kolisi, in the partners' suite when Siya went on. I nudged him and pointed to Siya running on, and his reaction was one of pure pride and joy. Earlier, I had fetched him from Nelspruit Airport and it took tremendous effort to get him to the game as his leg was in plaster and he was on crutches. Though he couldn't stand, Siya's dad pumped his arms and cheered loudly.

'The ball just kept coming to me,' Siya said after the match. 'It was a tough Test and we were behind and Jean rallied the guys and said we had to score next. But we didn't and Scotland scored and I just felt panic. Jean just laughed, given his previous speech to us. It broke the tension and we came back and won the game. I asked him afterwards why he laughed and he said he couldn't show the team how much he was panicking. I learned a big lesson from Jean that day when it comes to captaincy.'

I don't think Siya thought that his captaincy would be put to the test quite like it was in those first 20 minutes against England, which were madness with England scoring three tries to lead 24-3 and I just couldn't believe that 20 minutes after that it was half-time and we were ahead 29-27.

I just felt adrenaline all throughout that Test and absolute relief that we were ahead when the final whistle went. We won 42-39 and my immediate memory of the match is Sbu Nkosi scoring two tries and Faf de Klerk was just everywhere and named the Man of the Match.

I will never forget Rassie and Siya's smile in the change room because not only had they beaten England at Ellis Park, but such a weight seemed to have been lifted off them as the performance and result backed up everything Rassie had been saying.

It was a precursor of what was to come in Japan 18 months later, with 10 or so players from each side at it again in the World Cup final and, in 2018, it made for a pleasurable week in Bloemfontein, where the second Test was played.

Sometimes you don't want to read the newspapers or go online after a Test match, but this time I wanted to read everything that was said about the Springboks and the occasion and I wanted to know how our media felt, compared to the media in the United Kingdom. They were all in agreement that it had been a great Test match and that it had been made even more memorable because of the history attached to it for South African rugby.

Eddie was magnanimous after the Test and he popped into our change room to congratulate Rassie, Siya and the team. He was complimentary when speaking to the media afterwards and said that, while England were disappointed to lose, it was a great result for South Africa as a country.

I felt on a high, but the last line in the South African *Sunday Times* match report was a reminder not to get too carried away. I read: 'The Boks could breathe easy ... for now.'

It felt like more of a warning than 'well done' and was another example of how tough the rugby media are in South Africa and that you are only ever as good as your last Test. No matter how big the win or the occasion, the message was clear – this was a team that needed to win if they didn't want to spend the next 18 months feeling out of breath and anxious all the time.

That night, if my heart rate was up or I was short of breath it was out of excitement because I couldn't think of a greater gift from the Springboks to the late Nelson Mandela. This was the kind of day that he was referring to whenever he said sport had the power to unite and, in our country's context, the Springboks had the power to unite the nation.

On this night at Ellis Park I felt at home and at one with South Africa as a rainbow nation and united country, and everyone felt the same way – the players celebrated a win that the next day would be written about as being bigger than a rugby result.

Ellis Park has been home to so many good times for me with the Springboks. There is just something so different about playing there for the players than when playing anywhere else in South Africa. The FNB Stadium was a 'wow' experience because we played the All Blacks in front of a crowd of nearly 100 000, and Newlands in Cape Town, Loftus Versfeld in Pretoria, Kings Park in Durban, Port Elizabeth's Boet Erasmus Stadium and Nelson Mandela Bay Stadium all had their own particular charm. But Ellis Park, for the Springboks, is the equal of what playing at Eden Park is for the All Blacks. It is a fortress and I always got the feeling the players felt they could not lose there and the opposition always seemed to doubt if it was possible that they could win there.

My first Springbok win against the All Blacks also came at Ellis Park, in 2004, a night that was extra special because my brother, Mike, was in the stands. Marius Joubert scored three tries and we won 40-26.

We had lost narrowly that year in New Zealand and Jake was clear in his message to the players afterwards. He had told them that, in that match, by the time they believed they were good enough to beat the All Blacks in New Zealand, it was too late. He challenged the players to take what they then knew into the rematch at Ellis Park because as he and John would often say, it was one thing to hope and another to know.

The Springbok players on that day knew they could win, and win they did. It felt so good to be a part of a Springbok team beating the All Blacks after the experience of having lost to them eight times in succession between 2001 and the away Test in 2004.

After the win in Hamilton in 2009, it would again be a long wait to experience that rare feeling of beating the All Blacks in New Zealand. For the better part of the next decade I felt like I had gone back to the future in getting so close but being so far whenever we played the All Blacks.

Ironically, we twice lost matches against the All Blacks because of missed penalty kicks from two of the best in Louis Koen and Morné Steyn. It was as if the rugby gods weren't going to do us any favours and it didn't help that, from 2010 to 2015, New Zealand fielded one of the greatest All Blacks teams ever to play the game – although we were not far off beating them. The average score in the eight Tests between the two countries when Heyneke Meyer coached the Springboks was 27-18 to the All Blacks, and when the two teams played for the final time under Heyneke in the 2015 World Cup semi-final at Twickenham in London, the All Blacks won 20-18.

Losing to the All Blacks, whether by one point or conceding 57 points (as had happened to us twice in 2016 and 2017) had become a habit, and when Rassie took over he targeted beating the All Blacks in Wellington, New Zealand, in 2018. He said there was no such thing as a good defeat against the All Blacks, or any team for that matter, and that the only way to earn their respect was to beat them. They would only fear the Springboks if we beat them regularly.

Rassie's messaging in the first few months in 2018 was similar to Jake's message to the players in 2004 as both coaches kept on challenging the players to define a performance that would make them believe they could win the World Cup.

In 2004, the Springboks faced Ireland in Bloemfontein in Jake's first match in charge. He asked the players before the game what chance they gave themselves of beating the All Blacks in New Zealand if they were worried about losing to Ireland in Bloemfontein. The Boks won in Bloemfontein and then beat Ireland again in Cape Town but just lost (23-21) in New Zealand. Jake's message was that we had shown we were too good to lose to anyone at Ellis Park, including the All Blacks, and that was the feeling I got from within the camp in the week of the 40-26 win at Ellis Park in 2004.

I got a similar sense in 2018 that the belief would turn into a Test-winning performance. Rassie's team built every week for the Test against the All Blacks in Wellington, which could possibly have contributed to the narrow defeat against the Wallabies in Brisbane a week before the All Blacks match.

When I say the players tend to find something extra in the build-up to an All Blacks match, it's not that they were underprepared for the Test against Australia in Brisbane. But if you had asked them which win would have greater significance, the answer would have been the All Blacks in Wellington, because they were world champions and we had won once in 12 Tests against them between 2012 and 2017.

Rassie was emphatic before the Test against Australia, and even after the 23-18 defeat, that we would beat the All Blacks, and the players arrived in Wellington confident that they could do it. I had travelled enough with the Springboks to differentiate between false bravado and a genuine belief and what I was experiencing in Wellington in 2018 was exactly what I had felt with the Springboks when we were in New Zealand in 2008 and 2009. I knew we could win, Rassie and the coaches knew they could win and each time I interacted with the players that week I just got more confident that it would happen.

But then we were in New Zealand and we were playing the All Blacks and I had been there enough times to know that you only really know when you hear the final whistle and double check the scoreboard to make sure you are still ahead. The Wellington match tested my nerves, forced me to make use of the whisky flask more than I wanted to and, with just a few minutes to go, I got that awful feeling that we were going to lose when at one stage we were comfortably ahead. Then the All Blacks scored to make it 34-36 and I just couldn't bear to watch the conversion kick. I was convinced it was going to go over and that, at 36-36, they would have the momentum in the final few minutes and our change room afterwards would be one of heartbreak.

Well, history will tell you Beauden Barrett hit the post with the conversion and our guys tackled themselves to a standstill defending the tryline for the final two minutes before the All Blacks knocked on. It was the most nerve-wracking final two minutes I had known – even more so than in Hamilton in 2009 when Dan Carter's cross-kick momentarily threatened to turn into a New Zealand match-winning try – but when that final whistle went it was also right up there with what I had felt in Dunedin in 2008 and Hamilton in 2009. We had done it and everything that Rassie had spoken about in Washington DC and Johannesburg in that first week of June had come to fruition. We had beaten the All Blacks in New Zealand and the players knew they were good enough to win the World Cup.

I had been in the change room for the final few minutes, watching on TV and, with seconds to go, Rassie came running in – he'd left the coaching box early to get past the crowd before the final whistle. We watched the final knock-on together and when the final whistle went, he picked me up and swung me round in elation.

Winning in New Zealand is the pinnacle for the Springboks, but winning against England at Twickenham also has a very special place in the hearts of the Springboks, and my utopia moment at Twickenham came with Peter de Villiers' Springboks in 2008.

I love the occasion at Twickenham because it does feel like you are playing at the home of rugby. It is all so civilised and proper and professional in the build-up to any Test against England. The RFU are a pleasure to work with, staying in London is always a treat for me and I got along very well with those who worked at the RFU and were linked to the England team.

Any visit to London is one I love, but this visit with the Springboks was unmatched because of the team environment, the quality of the players, the joy we got from being in each other's company and the sublime performance in beating England 42-6 in what remains South Africa's biggest win at Twickenham.

I was so chuffed for Peter, Dick Muir, Gary Gold and the players because it was a perfect performance and just reward for the effort of everyone involved. It was also the perfect response to Peter's critics.

While Peter, like all Bok coaches, certainly had his critics, my experience of the coach was that he created a positive working environment for the management team and one in which I prospered, and the players were empowered to produce performances like that one at Twickenham, which set the tone for a 2009 season in which the team beat the All Blacks three times and won the series against the British & Irish Lions.

Schalk Brits – Bok captain

Annelee, the one and only!

How do I even start to write something about such an incredible woman, friend, and so much more?

Annelee is so dedicated and has sacrificed so much for her friends, the Springboks and ultimately our beloved country, South Africa.

For so many years, you were the glue and the go-to person, whatever the issue. It is because of the way in which you fulfilled that role that you can look back at a career and know that you have made many friends along the way.

Thank you for looking after all of us, and for also having the heart and taking the time to help with our other halves.

Thank you, thank you, thank you!

Chapter 13

THE BAD ...

There was absolute devastation on John Smit's face when he came off the field at Suncorp Stadium in Brisbane, Australia, on 15 July 2006. He looked haunted and that image is something I will never forget. The Wallabies had beaten us 49-0.

Watching it unfold was so surreal because there was nothing in the build-up to suggest there would be such a blowout or capitulation. The year before that we had won in Perth and beaten Australia three times in succession, and we'd started the 2006 season positively with two wins against Scotland in South Africa.

We had lost for the first time under Jake White at Newlands a fortnight before leaving for Australia, which had surprised Jake and John and I guess everyone in the squad, especially because we were ahead at half-time and everything seemed to be going right. But there were no red flags to warn us that something even more devastating was waiting in Australia, like not scoring a point and conceding nearly 50 points.

It was Pierre Spies and Akona Ndungane's debut that night, and what would usually be an occasion to celebrate was overshadowed by the result.

Jake was also crushed and he locked himself in the toilet cubicle a few minutes before the end to escape the madness of the moment and to try and get back his composure. I knocked on the door repeatedly for him to come out, but he wouldn't. I knew he had media commitments, so I lifted my head up over the door and looked down and saw he was in tears. In that moment, Jake was broken.

When he decided to come out of the cubicle, he was a different person and waited for the players to get to the change room. Words would never do justice to the hollowness of the mood, and Jake waited for all the players and management to get inside before he called everyone into a huddle. He spoke with such hope and conviction, and he took the players back to the scene of his first Test in charge in 2004 when we played Ireland in Bloemfontein.

That afternoon in Bloemfontein before the match, Jake had told the players to imagine the World Cup trophy in the middle of the huddle because it was going to be a reality. He told the players that they would win the World Cup in 2007 and that the bulk of those players who were going to do it were in the change room on that day in 2004. He had constantly taken the players back to the huddle in Bloemfontein and the visualisation of the World Cup being in that huddle.

He had told the players that they could expect a roller-coaster ride over the next four years and that there would be great moments but there would also be difficult post-mortems because no team was going to win every Test match. He told them to believe, work hard and never give up on the dream of winning the World Cup. We beat Ireland that day and would beat them a week later in Cape Town, but in Brisbane two years later, we were a squad who had just experienced a thrashing.

In the change room afterwards, Jake didn't speak about the match, all he spoke about was the World Cup trophy. He told the players that the feeling of getting nil and conceding 49 points would stick with them forever, but he also said it had to be consigned to history and that the players would be back in Australia in a fortnight and they would get the chance to redeem themselves. He urged them to do themselves proud in the next match against the All Blacks in New Zealand and to show the world that what had just happened was an aberration and not representative of this or any other Springbok team. The players were better than the score and they knew that because they had beaten Australia three times in 2005.

Jake was massive in that moment and I will never forget wondering how he had turned himself around so quickly from that crushed figure behind a closed toilet door. It showed me how mentally strong Jake was and that year he and John would both have to be because, in the next few months, I would experience and observe the type of pressure within a Springbok squad that I wouldn't see again until 2016.

What made 2016 slightly more bearable was that we had been struggling all season, but in 2006, leading into the Brisbane disaster, this was a Springbok team that had won a lot more than they had lost, and that had beaten the All Blacks at home in 2004 and 2005 and came so close to repeating in 2006. We were not a bad team and one match didn't make us a bad team – the guys fought hard in the remaining Tests to beat Australia and New Zealand in South Africa and, one year later, won the World Cup in France.

When I think of my worst Test match days in 20 years, Brisbane is there for the result – and for how shattered Jake and John were straight after the match – but it was also a Saturday evening where I saw every leadership quality in the Bok coach and captain as they looked to rebuild players and management who felt like they had been hit by a train.

I didn't think it could ever get worse for a Springbok team or that I would ever feel as low as I did that night in Brisbane in 2006, but it happened again in 2017 against the All Blacks at the North Harbour Stadium in Albany, just outside of Auckland. The All Blacks won 57-0 and it seemed like I was watching a re-run of that night at Suncorp Stadium. I just couldn't believe it and I spent the match going between the change room and the side of the field, and each time I looked up the score was getting worse. It was the most desperate I had felt after a Test match and I found myself in the change room a few minutes before the end whistle, alone in a corner in tears. I don't cry at rugby matches but these were tears of pain and desperation. I had seen what Jake, John and the squad had endured in 2006 as they fought their way back and, while it was admirable, I didn't wish that type of pressure on anyone.

Coach Allister Coetzee and captain Eben Etzebeth were numb. The players were stunned and the change room was silent. No one said anything. There was to be no inspirational moment in the change room that night. The North Harbour Stadium change rooms are directly opposite each other and only three metres apart and we could hear the All Blacks singing and celebrating a record win against South Africa.

The tradition that developed between international teams over the years is that the host team invites the visitors over to their change room for a beer and a chat, and this became commonplace because of the phasing out of post-match functions, which was mainly down to the late kick-offs.

I remember our players not wanting to go across, and why would they? I didn't want to be in the All Blacks' change room and I didn't think the All Blacks players would want to be having a chat with our guys, given what had just happened. There is such a respect between the two groups of players and, no matter the result, there has always been a graciousness and humility from both sides. The Springboks' rivalry with the All Blacks is on another level to any other team that we play. There is always an extra edge in the camp before an All Blacks Test, and that goes up a level when it is in New Zealand, which made this night just so horrible.

When we finally summoned the energy as a group to step into the All Blacks' change room to congratulate them and share a drink, their response overwhelmed me. They quietened down their celebrations for those few minutes, put on hold the euphoria they were feeling, and players from both sides – who over the years had come to know each other well from playing in Super Rugby – had a drink together. All Blacks coach Steve Hansen, who I had known from the days when he coached New Zealand U20 in South Africa, was the first to greet me. He came over with a beer in his hand, gave me a hug and said, 'It will get better, you are too good a side for it not to'.

Steve would remind me of that moment at the 2019 World Rugby Awards, which were held the night after we won the World Cup. I caught his eye when we arrived and he immediately came over and congratulated me. 'I told you it would get better,' he said. 'You guys really deserved it.'

The relationship between the Springboks and All Blacks is something special and it is the one opposition jersey the players covet and the one Test match they want to play in, especially in New Zealand.

As you can imagine, I have collected a lot of memorabilia over the years, but the only opposition jersey that I have framed is an All Blacks jersey I received in 2005 from Shandy (Darren Shand), the long-standing team manager.

The players want to face the haka and experience it in front of the New Zealand home crowd and every player will tell you it is a career highlight. For me, it was always memorable and in my 28 visits to New Zealand, I never got bored with the pre-match ritual and the occasion of the Springboks playing the All Blacks.

I was also very blessed to be part of a Springbok team that beat the All Blacks in New Zealand in successive years and those victories remain right up there with the World Cup triumphs.

Wellington, New Zealand, would also be where I experienced my worst World Cup moment when we lost 11-9 to the Wallabies in a quarter-final we remember as one of the most controversial matches in World Cup history.

It is not for me to comment on the refereeing of Bryce Lawrence, in his last match, but the players and coaches really felt they had been done a dirty and it was such an awful way to end a campaign in which the belief of defending the World Cup had become stronger with each week.

Springbok coach Peter de Villiers had introduced Rassie Erasmus and Jacques Nienaber to his World Cup coaching team and they slotted in seamlessly with assistant coaches Dick Muir and Gary Gold. Peter was brilliant in managing their integration. It was also his management style to empower the senior players like John, Victor Matfield, Fourie du Preez and Schalk Burger and there was such optimism in the build-up to the quarter-final. But afterwards it felt like we had lost so much more than a rugby match. It felt like the passing of an era, where so many of the players who had won the World Cup in 2007 and beaten the British & Irish Lions in 2009 had come to the end of their international careers.

None of them had confirmed that they would not play Test rugby beyond the 2011 World Cup, and neither had Peter suggested he would not be available to continue, but there was this sense of loss back at the team hotel and that something very special had come to an end.

Pat Lambie – Bok captain

AL, thank you for pouring your heart and soul into the happiness and well-being of all of us for so many years.

Everyone around you felt like they were always receiving special treatment and being especially looked after.

Nothing was ever too much to ask, or too far out of your reach or capacity – requests for dozens of extra tickets at venues all over the world for families and friends, and friends of friends; golf bookings at the most iconic courses; tickets to the most exciting events; passport renewals and visa application approvals in a matter of days (sometimes even hours).

AL, you effortlessly mixed it with our young girlfriends, our older wives, our parents and grandparents, our babies and children, all with the same delightful manner.

You treated everyone fairly and with respect, and although so friendly, we knew never to mess with you, the strongest individual in the Springbok camp at any given time over your period of service.

You have been the backbone of the South African rugby family. Your incredible legacy is one that will be spoken of forever, and is impossible to replicate.

I can't wait to read what lies in the pages of this book!

Chapter 14

THE UGLY

Losing to Australia in Wellington, New Zealand, in the 2011 World Cup quarter-finals ranks among my bad Springbok memories, but it also is among the ones I describe as ugly though this has nothing to do with the performance or the result.

There was such a belief in the Springbok squad that it was possible to defend the World Cup and to have beaten the All Blacks in New Zealand at the 2011 World Cup would have been the ultimate accolade. The players were angry afterwards and the coaches were as angry, but for the likes of myself and the rest of the management team we had to put all the emotion aside and make sure we adhered to World Rugby's World Cup regulations that the entire squad exit the tournament and the country within 24 hours of losing in the quarter-finals.

We had planned for both scenarios, although the one that I was praying for was a flight to Auckland for the semi-final and not the one that meant spending the early hours of Sunday morning managing the process of the squad heading home on different flights, via different countries, because the remoteness of New Zealand meant there was limited capacity.

Percy Montgomery still teases operations chief Charles Wessels about how long it took his flight to arrive in Johannesburg. Monty was in the group that had left New Zealand first, and they arrived at the same time as the group that had left 20 hours later. For the group of players who were travelling with me, it got even worse because we had to spend eight hours at Sydney Airport to catch a connecting flight that went Hong Kong-Dubai-Johannesburg. And no matter where we looked there seemed to be a television report or newspaper headline of the Wallabies' win.

We met up with the Ireland team in Dubai, who were transferring to Dublin – they had left the tournament after us. Fourie du Preez, Danie

Rossouw, Gurthrö Steenkamp and Pierre Spies were among the players who had travelled on my flight, and they were not impressed.

It couldn't have been an easy job for World Rugby to plan a number of exit scenarios from a remote location, but in the moment we just could not see past our exhaustion and disappointment.

It had been difficult to escape New Zealand and I knew that there wouldn't be much escape once we got home because I doubted the media and rugby public were in any way going to be sympathetic to the manner of our defeat.

That night of the 2011 World Cup quarter-final defeat ranks so highly on my Springbok lows because the end result had nothing to do with a lack of performance or not being good enough; the way we lost and the way we went out of the tournament just seemed so wrong. There were many great players in the squad who would retire from international rugby after the tournament and, as I would find out so often, there was seldom a fairy-tale ending to careers and when one did come along, it was more the exception than the norm.

One fairy-tale ending that springs to mind is Bakkies Botha, who retired on his own terms after the win against England at Twickenham in 2014.

The 53-3 defeat against England at Twickenham in 2002 is also banked among the ugly for me, not so much because we lost but because of the manner of our defeat. The coach, Rudolf Straeuli, had selected a lot of youngsters for the three tour matches and we had lost to France in Marseilles and Scotland in Edinburgh, so no one gave us a realistic chance of beating an England team that was considered to be the best in the world.

Twickenham is a daunting place to play, even when you arrive in England with a very good team, so it was a nervous week. The change room looked like a hospital afterwards, the players were a mess and Rudolf had a blank expression on his face. He just couldn't bring himself to front the media immediately after the final whistle for the coach's interview and the broadcaster kept on insisting that they needed the coach and captain. I tried to explain that in the circumstance the team needed some quiet time and pleaded for some understanding, but had to push the coach and captain to honour the broadcast contract obligations. Eventually Corné Krige, as captain, did the television post-match interview and Rudolf addressed the media at the post-match press conference. It wasn't nice to watch him get a grilling from the media and to make it even worse the accusations of Corné knocking out André Pretorius, albeit accidentally, were true.

The incident summed up our trip and a tour that had started with such enthusiasm because of the youthful make-up of the squad, but it went downhill very quickly. We lost against France in Marseilles where Jean de Villiers' Test debut was ended with a knee-ligament injury in the first five minutes, and it never got any better the following Saturday in Edinburgh against Scotland. The team was always on the back foot, the media pressure was intense and it didn't matter how we tried to turn negatives into positives, by the time the team arrived in London, we were on a hiding to nothing.

I mentioned earlier that it also coincided with Mark Shuttleworth, the South African tech billionaire, handing out the jerseys for the match against England. Mark was generous in his praise for the Springboks when he spoke to the team – he spoke about his experience of turning a dream into reality, and how even though the odds were stacked against a young Bok team, anything was possible.

I don't quite know which Test match or moment to rank as the ugliest during my time with the Springboks, but when I think of those ugly afternoons or nights, I think of the South African supporter Piet van Zyl somehow breaking through security at Kings Park in Durban in 2002 and trying to tackle Irish referee Dave McHugh. It was an awful moment for me, and I am sure every Springbok supporter, to see this person wearing an old Bok jersey embarrass South Africa.

What made it worse was that he ran on at a time when we were leading the All Blacks and our players were clearly comfortable in the way Dave was interpreting things. In that moment I just knew what our night and week would be like off the field and that it wouldn't matter what happened in the rest of the match, myself and the media manager were going to be the busiest people. And so we were, dealing with every different type of enquiry and protest, and in the days that followed you would have thought it was a Springbok player who had assaulted the referee.

The team was furious with what had happened and disgusted that this person would call themselves a Bok supporter and actually think what he did was in any way helping the team. It was a very dark day for South Africa.

Where I take full responsibility for an ugly Bok night was in Toulouse in 2009, with the infamous Ras Dumisani anthem performance. What an embarrassing shambles.

I take great pride in our national anthem and I love singing it. In the early years, I was responsible for appointing the anthem singer, but SA Rugby's tours department took over when my involvement with the Boks grew.

The players love the anthem and also take a huge interest in who sings it. We've had such incredible performers of the national anthem over the years, with Claire Johnston, South African tenor Bongani Tembe, Hugh Masekela, Lira, Bobby van Jaarsveld, Sipho 'Hotstix' Mabuse, Yvonne Chaka Chaka, Kurt Darren, Nianell, the Coleske Brothers and Zolani Mahola, the lead singer of Freshly Ground, who sang the anthem the night of Siya's debut as captain at Ellis Park on 9 June 2018.

Charlotte Church sang the South African anthem beautifully in Cardiff, Katherine Jenkins also sang the anthem in Wales, the Scotland military band mainly played in Edinburgh and opera singer Camilla Kerslake, the wife of former England captain Chris Robshaw, was amazing at Twickenham. Springbok flanker Heinrich Brüssow's wife, Caroline, was also inspiring in singing the anthem before the second Test against England in 2018, when we trailed 12-0 after 10 minutes and ended up winning 23-12.

There have been some superstar performances and it is because SA Rugby give such significance to who performs the national anthems of both teams. The anthem performance overseas was part of my portfolio and, usually, I was involved from the outset to the end in the process, but on this particular occasion the French Rugby Federation had arranged with the South African Embassy and said they had already picked the performer. They had given the embassy an assurance of the quality of the performer and the embassy had informed me that Ras Dumisani would be performing our anthem. None of us had heard of him and, even though the French insisted everything would be OK, it troubled me and I should have done more to get a meeting with him to hear his rendition. Instead, I only had a brief introduction where Ras described himself as a Durban-born reggae singer who now lived in Marseilles, and he seemed confident and excited.

Goodness, what a disaster. The moment the players lined up and saw him and two bongo-drummers, I got some very puzzled looks. For the singing of the anthem, the management line up on the field opposite the players, and the moment he started to destroy the anthem with his version, the players' eyes all seemed to focus on me. Schalk Burger's expression was one of 'WTF' and I was thinking exactly the same thing.

The Guardian newspaper described it as 'not just bad but not-knowing-where-to-look bad.' It was a night that had started disastrously and ended no better as we lost 20-13 to France.

As proud South Africans we always took pride in the privilege of being able to sing the national anthem. From when I joined the Springboks we always ensured every player knew the anthem and for those over the years who didn't, they learned it immediately when they came into the squad.

Ard Matthews, former lead singer of Just Jinger, was also in the middle of another anthem misfire. Having performed the team song, 'Fire', at the announcement of the 2011 World Cup squad, Ard reluctantly accepted a very late request to perform the anthem live on television – it quickly became evident that he wasn't prepared, and he forgot the words to the anthem. As I had felt for Ras, I felt terrible for Ard.

National anthems aside, an afternoon that started with an on-field disaster was when Ireland's South African-born flanker CJ Stander knocked out Pat Lambie with an illegal challenge at Newlands in June 2016. CJ was making his Test debut and 22 minutes into the match he leapt into the air and his hips collided with Pat's head. It was a sickening moment. I knew instantly that Pat was in trouble and it was one of those matches where my focus was on the health of a player and I have very little recollection of the Test itself.

Pat's wife, Kate, and I were in the partners' suite in the Jan Pickard Stand and we raced down to meet his parents at the players' entrance. I took them into the medical room to see Pat. CJ, who had been red-carded in the incident, was in the Ireland change room and he came into the medical room in tears.

Pat was very dazed but acknowledged everyone and wanted to know what the score was before he went to the hospital. CJ was distraught and he wanted to know whether Pat was OK. The head injury assessment protocols meant that I had to clear the room and let the medical professionals do their job.

I spent the rest of the match reassuring Kate and the Lambies that Pat was in the best possible hands before they went off to join him at the hospital.

Pat is the type of person every mom and dad would want their daughter to bring home. He was such a treat to work with because he has such a balanced outlook on life and never lived in the bubble that often comes with being a Springbok. He was among the most popular players at a Bok signing session and spent a lot of his off-time studying to complete a degree while playing international rugby, which was very rare among players who often focused exclusively on their rugby careers as their profession.

Pat was measured, calm and a bit of a silent assassin in how he could destroy teams and he was very highly rated within the squad, by the players and also the coaches. His winning penalty against the All Blacks at Ellis Park in 2014, from more than 50 metres and with the last kick of the game, was a measure of his ability to deal with pressure.

I always marvel at the composure of the flyhalves I've worked with – nothing ever seemed to faze the likes of Pat, Morné Steyn, Butch James, André Pretorius, Elton Jantjies and Handré Pollard. Flyhalf is a position that requires players to take control and remain cool, calm and collected. These guys epitomised that unique No 10 characteristic.

Unfortunately, no amount of composure could save Pat from the effects of a series of head knocks and his rugby career ended prematurely. He made just five more appearances for South Africa after the collision with CJ.

I felt awful for Pat that afternoon and, though I was initially upset with CJ, I was emotionally moved when I read about his remorse in an article. I know that Pat has put this incident down to rugby being a physical game with injuries part and parcel of it.

Ireland won that match 26-20 to clinch their first win on South African soil and, unfortunately, this wasn't the only time that the Boks suffered historic losses in my time with the team – there were two occasions in 244 matches when I just did not consider it a possibility that we would lose.

The first was against Japan at the 2015 World Cup and I just couldn't believe how the game was unfolding and how all the momentum was with Japan. Fourie du Preez, who had played for Eddie Jones at Top League club Suntory Sungoliath in Japan before the World Cup, had been so vocal about the threat of Japan. He had tried to warn the team not to underestimate Japan and not to think of them as an inferior rugby nation. He told the squad that this was the match Eddie and the Japan team had spent four years preparing for, and that he knew Eddie well enough to know that they would seriously be up for this challenge and we had better bring our A-game.

In hindsight, we weren't on our A-game and Japan played the most incredible of matches to beat us in the last movement of the game. I couldn't bring myself to watch the final few phases of play and I made my way towards the tunnel leading to our change room. As I was walking away from the field, I heard the roar of the very pro-Japan crowd and turned to face the field and the stands where I had just come from. I got a glimpse of South African businessman Johann Rupert and his wife Gaynor and he looked haunted by what he was watching unfold. Johann is one of the most ardent supporters of South Africa and was incredibly caring and kind to me during my tenure – a wise mind, he would often call simply to encourage me and check in. From the look on his face, I knew right away the roar at the stadium wasn't good news for the Springboks. I quickly hastened my walk and made my way to the change room.

Fourie was one of the first players back in the change room and I have never seen him so angry. There was a long narrow corridor that led to the change room and Fourie was cursing the whole way there, absolutely furious because what had happened was everything that he had warned us about. That was not a nice change room to be in afterwards, and neither was the one in Florence on 19 November 2016 when the Springboks lost for the first time in history against Italy.

I should have learned after the Japan experience but I did not think Italy could ever beat the Springboks. It just so happened to come at the end of a week that should have been one of the best in my career with the Springboks because we were based in the beautiful city of Florence, it was to be my 200th Test and the 100th Test for my good friend, Daliah Hurwitz, the Bok massage therapist.

Selfishly, this was a week made in heaven for me. I am a lover of food and travel and to be in Florence was one big indulgence because the rugby media in Italy is a lot less intense than in England, New Zealand, Ireland and Wales. In between my duties, there was time to go sightseeing, taste exquisite food and enjoy the fine wines.

Having said that, the week didn't start stress-free. Captain Adriaan Strauss and I had stayed in London on the Sunday to attend the World Rugby Awards, hosted by Princess Charlene of Monaco, while the team were en route to Florence. I'd just arrived at the awards venue when I received a call to advise me that Jamba Ulengo had been denied a boarding pass as he didn't have a Shengen visa. Jamba was dispatched to our hotel where he bunked with Adriaan that night. The next 12 hours were an example of the rugby community rallying – the president of Italian rugby was at the awards ceremony on Sunday night, he put me in touch with the Italian Embassy in London who assisted us early on Monday morning by issuing a visa, and just like that Jamba and I were in Florence before the first training session.

The match in Florence was one occasion where I didn't think I would need to work the whisky flask, but it was nearly empty by the end of the game, which we lost 20-18.

It was a change room I didn't want to be in afterwards because the players were embarrassed as much as hurt and you could see they felt they had let themselves down. I really felt sorry for the coach, Allister Coetzee, because he just seemed helpless to stem the tide or turn things around.

I had worked with Allister when he was Jake's assistant coach between 2004 and 2007 and always enjoyed his company, but being an assistant coach cannot compare to the pressures of being the head coach. Allister took a lot of strain and I have never seen a coach that psychologically beaten as I did that night. I had seen coaches at their lowest and most vulnerable over the years, but that night he was a combination of drained and defeated.

What made the night even worse was that the Italians still hosted an after-match dinner, which is a gala experience. The afternoon kick-off allowed for a high-quality official evening, but if ever there was one night in Florence where myself and the team could have done without the Italian hospitality, the incredible food and the best wines, it was that night as Italy celebrated the biggest win in their rugby history. Our players were to be admired for the way they behaved at the dinner because it was the last place they would ever have wanted to be. The moment we got back to the team hotel, Adriaan called the senior players together and off they went to figure out what had happened and how to make sure it never happened again.

It was a very strange end to a Test match night because the players had called their own crisis meeting and the management duties had to go on, no matter how down everyone was feeling. There was still one match to be played on tour, but it was hard to go to Cardiff in the wake of this loss and prepare for a Test match against Wales. We suffered a record 27-13 loss before a long flight home after a difficult tour.

If that was rugby ugly, it doesn't get worse than what happened in 2004. Unrelated to the Boks, my worst experience came when South Africa hosted the 2004 U19 World Cup tournament in Durban. During Ireland's opening match against New Zealand, flanker John McCall collapsed.

I was on the side of the field at the time, as I had been assigned to assist the teams at the tournament. After John collapsed, I could tell by the reaction of the emergency medical staff that this was very serious.

John was only 18 when he succumbed to heart failure in what was the saddest day of my career.

I worked closely with Ireland U19 team manager Michael Cunningham, as SA Rugby flew the McCall family out from Ireland, and I flew to Joburg to meet and accompany them to Durban. I have stayed in touch with the family over the years and visited them during my stint with World Rugby in Ireland.

Taking John's parents to the funeral home after such a tragic event reminded me that rugby is really just a sport, and that there is so much more to life.

Adriaan Strauss – Bok captain

Wow, what an amazing woman! Not only do all her records speak for themselves, but she changed and shaped the lives of the people she encountered.

My first call-up to play for the Springboks was in 2008 against Australia in Perth. It was a bit late in the week after an injury, but I was as excited as a six-year-old boy on Christmas Day when I arrived at Johannesburg Airport, only to realise I'd left my visa in my temporary passport, which was still in my flat in Bloemfontein.

Never having met Annelee, I reluctantly called her for help. She was already in Perth but she listened as I explained my problem. Within 20 minutes, she called back and told me to sit tight.

She had somehow managed to get hold of a spare key to my flat, arranged for someone to search my very untidy flat for the passport, then organised that my mom would take it to the airport and give it to a pilot that Annelee had spoken to, and who would be on the next flight to Johannesburg. He hand-delivered my visa to me at the airport!

Because of Annelee, I made it to Perth in time to do the captain's run on the Friday and played in my first Test.

If you want something done, and done right, who you gonna call? Annelee Murray.

Chapter 15

FROM BARB WIRE TO BOKTOWN

The loyalty of South African fans to the Springboks is matched by the loyalty of sponsors to the Springboks, regardless of the result. This is what I learnt from the experience of doing almost 200 Springbok sponsors shoots and attending five World Cups in two decades with the team.

Naturally, it was that much easier when we were winning consistently and when the Springboks carried the tag of world champions, but even amid bleak years like 2016, there was so much kindness and goodwill towards the Springboks and SA Rugby.

Sponsorships are part of the marriage contract between professional sports and their commercial partners, and professional rugby can't survive without the investment of sponsors and the hope of long-term relationships. In the case of the Springboks, South African Breweries' Castle Lager has been the one constant since long before I joined SA Rugby in 2000. The Springboks' brand and sponsorship partners have included Sasol, Absa and, in the past few years, MTN, connecting fans around the world. These are all very strong South African brands that speak to the Bok supporters as much as the supporters speak to the sponsor products and services.

The Springboks have always been blessed with the type of sponsors who have invested, and I include SuperSport who, as the broadcast investor and partner have always been synonymous with the Springboks and every bit of emotion you would associate with the national rugby team.

I always appreciated working in this environment where there was so much sponsor and partner investment and support. Tsogo Sun, formerly the Southern Sun, are an incredible hotel partner who, like SuperSport, have been ever-present with every Springbok Test and World Cup campaign.

Unfortunately, in 2016 there was a short window between sponsorships that overlapped with one of the worst seasons in Springbok history.

Results were hard to come by, public support was low and Gavin Varejes stepped in as a short-term sponsor with his company, Blue Label Telecom. Gavin, despite all the negativity around the team and the beating we were taking in the media because of results, said he couldn't allow the Springboks to take the field without a jersey sponsor. As I have mentioned previously, Gavin is one of the biggest supporters of the Springboks and he has given so generously over the years. His love for rugby, which includes funding organisations such as the SA Rugby Legends and Rugby Centurions, is recognised among everyone in the game, and his passion was encapsulated in SA Rugby's #LoveRugby campaign to rally supporters around the game, regardless of the results.

It was this kind of national unity that was at the heart of the 2003 World Cup campaign. The 'Our Blood is Green' slogan was the work of the late Gary Grant, SA Rugby's head of commercial and marketing, and myself, communications manager Anthony Mackaiser and CEO Rian Oberholzer. All of us recognised the need to go beyond provincial rivalries that had become so strong during the years of rugby and sporting isolation.

'Our Blood is Green' was directed at every South African and every rugby supporter, with the message being that no matter your provincial affiliation, the one thing that unites all South Africans is the Springboks. It was a way of delivering the Springboks to South Africans as a national team and not one whose identity should be defined by their provincial teams or origins. The success of any emotive campaign is directly linked to the team's results, which for the early part of 2003 were promising.

We beat Scotland in two Tests, edged Argentina in Port Elizabeth and then won an incredible Test against the Wallabies at Newlands, with Brent Russell having one of those matches you never forget. He was everywhere and everything he touched turned to gold.

It should have been a highlight that gave us momentum to take on the All Blacks at Loftus Versfeld. The initial planning was that we would be based in Cape Town for the Wallabies Test at Newlands and then stay until the Thursday when we would fly to Johannesburg. But coach Rudolf Straeuli made a late change to the plans and suddenly moved our base to Durban.

The set schedule was the foundation of the week for many players and this change was disruptive because we only found out on the Saturday evening after beating Australia that we would be spending the week in Durban and not Cape Town. It was difficult from an organisational point of view because Rudolf had kept his plans close to his chest until the last moment.

Ultimately the coach is in charge and he did what he thought best. Keeping us on our toes was part of Rudolf's style but from a management point of view it was difficult to make sense of keeping the team in the dark.

Operational logistics, including flights and accommodation, are confirmed months in advance, and though this surprise disrupted the team, the silver lining was that the experience stretched us and taught us to be more adaptable.

Just as it seemed the Boks had turned the corner in 2003 with the win against Australia, everything flipped and a now infamous team-building camp plunged us into the fallout of a military-style operation. It wasn't pleasant and I was excluded from the planning of the camp. So many of us only learned what had happened after the fact.

My priority remained my job, which was the players, hosting their partners, accommodating SA Rugby's VIPs and doing the best possible job in giving the sponsors the type of relationship they would expect, given their investment in the Springboks.

It was a crazy build-up to the Test in Pretoria because Rudolf had flown in a team of provincial players to Durban to compete in a trial match against the Springboks. It was kept secret so that the media would not know, and even the Boks didn't know until they got to training.

The players were kept out of the loop of so many things in that week, as were management who were on a need-to-know basis. The team only found out they would not be staying at the Palazzo Hotel in Fourways when they got onto the bus at Johannesburg International Airport (changed to OR Tambo International Airport in 2006) on the Friday late afternoon. Instead, they'd be going to a location outside of Pretoria and wouldn't return until after the Test match.

The players were distracted by the sudden change to those things they usually took for granted, such as their match tickets being in order, the well-being of their wives, partners, kids and whoever they had invited to the Test match, and their usual Friday pre-Test rituals, which sometimes included having a catch-up with parents or a good friend at the team hotel. Players love routine and perform best when they know there is structure around those things that they have to do away from the playing field. I spent my Friday night and Saturday morning ensuring that the match tickets and accommodation were dealt with, and that their luggage had successfully made the trip from Durban and was waiting for them in a room at the Palazzo Hotel.

Rudolf's motivation was that he wanted to take them out of their comfort zone and mentally prepare them for the challenge of the All Blacks but unfortunately the result was that we lost 52-16.

Some of us had been invited to attend Nelson Mandela's 85th birthday celebration in Sandton after the match. The post-match obligations were rushed. Rudolf and captain Corné Krige were part of the group invited to the gala dinner and it was a scramble to get there on time because the dinner had started in Sandton soon after the Test match had ended in Pretoria. We were running late and I quickly had to make arrangements to get those partners who had opted to watch the match at the team hotel from the Palazzo to the Sandton venue.

Even though we were taken to the Convention Centre with a police escort, it didn't change the fact that we were late. We quietly made our way to the table, but there was a formal announcement that we had arrived and we were welcomed with generous applause. It was a sign of the love Mr Mandela had for the Springboks, but having the spotlight on us felt embarrassing after such a heavy defeat.

The evening was spectacular and the players were treated like celebrities, despite losing so heavily to the All Blacks. It was a bitter-sweet night for me personally as while I was so emotionally drained from the week's events and the result, I was also so inspired to be part of Mr Mandela's 85th birthday.

It was great to see Zelda, though she was in full work-mode, which I could relate to. The Irish family band, The Corrs performed live, Bono was there, as was former US president Bill Clinton, the Archbishop Desmond Tutu, Queen Beatrix of the Netherlands, former Zambian president Kenneth Kaunda, Oprah Winfrey and former South African president FW de Klerk. And so, in keeping with the humble spirit of Madiba, this high-profile gathering of 1 600 people included everyone from former presidents, to the Springboks to Madiba's personal chef and gardener. That night remains a big highlight for me even if the week was the opposite.

We still had to play Australia and New Zealand away from home and finish the Tri-Nations with a Test in Johannesburg against the Wallabies. That fortnight overseas was hard – we lost to Australia, Bakkies Botha was cited for foul play and later suspended, and it just seemed to be one crisis after the other. And to top it off, we still had to face the All Blacks in Dunedin.

Remarkably, we could actually have beaten the All Blacks that night and, so uncharacteristically, Louis Koen missed three penalties and a conversion in a game I remember mostly for prop Richard Bands running 40 metres to score a try and handing off All Blacks flyhalf Carlos Spencer.

The All Blacks won 19-11 and the mood in a Springbok change room is never good after a loss. There is no such thing as a good defeat, as I was once told by Springbok hooker Lukas van Biljon when I tried to take out the positives, but the competitiveness of the team seemed to have lifted morale and although we had an early flight to Sydney on the Sunday morning, and a long flight back to South Africa, there was a belief that we could be successful at the World Cup.

We had a great South African send-off to the World Cup in Australia, which included a farewell with Madiba. We were initially based in Perth for the opening two matches that included the big one against England.

In between losing 25-6 to England in Perth and 29-9 to the All Blacks in the Melbourne quarter-final, John Smit got his first taste of captaincy, Schalk Burger made his Test debut against Georgia in Sydney, and Derick Hougaard was flattened by Samoa centre Brian Lima in Brisbane.

I loved my first World Cup experience from a professional point of view and learned so much operationally, but personally and in the context of the team, I wish it had ended differently.

There was so much distraction and noise around the team, from the allegations of racism between Geo Cronjé and Quinton Davids at the World Cup preparation training camp in Pretoria to the infamous three-day Kamp Staaldraad (Camp Barb Wire) that followed the naming of the World Cup squad.

I didn't know that Kamp Staaldraad was going to happen and even when the players returned from the three-day bush camp to have a family weekend at the Drakensberg Sun, it was clear that whatever had happened was something they were not sharing with us. It was only after the World Cup that Corné, in his autobiography, wrote about the details of Kamp Staaldraad and confirmed what had been in the media.

It really was a tough time for the Springboks and through this the players tried to rally around this sense of national unity that had been inspired by the 'Our Blood is Green' campaign. We were desperate to do well at the 2003 World Cup but at the time I didn't have an idea of the trauma that had been caused by Kamp Staaldraad.

For me that World Cup will always be significant because it was the first that I was involved in. I experienced how different a World Cup is to playing one-off Tests, end-of-year tours, an inbound series to South Africa or competing in the Tri-Nations or Rugby Championship. World Cups bring a different kind of pressure to bear as the tournament places as much emphasis on the rugby as it does the promotion of the game through media engagements, and that didn't change in any of the subsequent four World Cups I was involved in.

The Springboks have a big following in Australia because of the ex-pat community, especially in Perth where we played England in the pool stage. Rian Oberholzer, Gary Grant and SA Rugby's Kyle Nel had launched BokTown for the first time, which was a massively popular Springbok-dedicated fans village. It was the first time something like this had been done at a World Cup and Perth was always going to be a winner because of the number of former South Africans living in Western Australia. Our match against England was also billed as one of the biggest matches of the pool stage but it did feel like those of us playing in Perth were detached from the World Cup, as everything seemed to be happening in Sydney and to a lesser degree Brisbane, which was a five-hour flight away.

BokTown was such a success that the South African initiative has evolved into 'RugbyTown' at each of the subsequent World Cups. Rian and I agreed that we needed to get Jean de Villiers and Gcobani Bobo, two members of the Bok World Cup squad who missed the event through injury, from South Africa to BokTown in Perth. They were thrust in front of the camera to do so many interviews and were a big hit with the fans. I like to think I pushed them into their post-rugby careers in broadcasting with SuperSport ... it's a pleasure, guys.

The Perth experience, in isolation, was great and South African businessman David Rodwell and his wife Rita were wonderful hosts and entertained the squad with a few braais. Being in Perth certainly allowed us to recreate a home atmosphere at BokTown and there was a lot of player and fan engagement. When the schedule allowed for it, we took the team to BokTown and it was like being at home, with boerewors rolls and Castle Lager being served. The challenge for BokTown came in the final fortnight when the playoffs took place in Sydney but the Boks had been eliminated from the tournament. There was a sense of despair because, as the Bok supporters were flying in to Sydney for the semi-finals, the team was flying out and back to South Africa.

The one thing about Springbok supporters is that they are particularly parochial in their support. If the Boks aren't playing in a tournament, then it is as if the event isn't taking place. The Springboks, as per the tournament rules, had to leave Australia but Rian had arranged for me to stay on in Sydney and manage BokTown, which now had more of an international flavour. Rugby supporters from all over still visited but the South African presence lacked what we had experienced in Perth, Brisbane and Sydney earlier in the tournament. I had spent a few days visiting Lisa Kingi-Bon in New Zealand, which gave me a mental break from the demands of those first five weeks, and I got back to Sydney feeling unburdened by being a neutral in the final week of the World Cup.

I also got to enjoy some time with two youngsters, Schalk Burger and Paul Delport, who had been nominated for World Rugby awards. Schalk had gone home with the squad but then returned 10 days later because of his nomination, and he would end up winning the tournament's best junior player award. Schalk, outside of the two years he missed from rugby while fighting an illness that nearly took his life, would always be a presence in the Springboks and one of those players who has never changed in personality from his first Test to the friend who appreciates a quality bottle of wine. Schalk and his wife Michele are close friends and we are pretty much neighbours in Cape Town.

Schalk epitomises everything that is special and respected about the Springboks. I know just how highly regarded he was by the opposition and the awe with which his teammates viewed him, and through it all, from his debut in 2003 to his international retirement in 2015, he has always just been Schalk.

When we watched the World Cup final in Sydney together as neutrals, I don't think either of us considered the 2007 World Cup, let alone imagined that we would be holding the trophy as winners. At that moment we just enjoyed the experience of being in the stands at a World Cup final and not caring who won, which seemed to be the general feeling among all those Springbok supporters we chatted to afterwards, who were dressed up in green but with no gold to show for it.

Warren Whiteley – Bok captain

It's difficult to describe the emotions one has when joining the Springboks for the first time. It's both exhilarating and frightening, a combination of feelings that can leave you in somewhat of a dream state.

I had many questions to ask after joining the squad as a late replacement in August 2014 but hadn't quite built up the courage to ask some of the senior management. I opted for the easier option by asking some of my teammates.

The one name that frequently arose was Annelee. 'Just ask AL.'

I soon realised that Annelee was an integral part of the Springboks, responsible for a variety of tasks. Simply put, if there was anything you needed, AL was the go-to.

With the experience of almost 250 Test matches including five World Cups and two World Cup wins, Annelee encompasses everything that the Springboks stand for.

Her dedication, love and passion will be shared amongst many a player for years to come!

SuperSport
World of Champions

PREVIOUS PAGE: Holding the 2019 Hollard Sports Personality Award in Joburg.
ABOVE: At the 2015 Laureus World Sports Awards in Shanghai with Jean, Schalk and Shaun.
TOP RIGHT: Jean's 100th Test in Wellington, 2014.
BOTTOM RIGHT: My friends, Toks and Kobus.

SPRINGBOK
100th Test
ABS
SPRINGBOK

ABOVE: Eben's 50th Test in Brisbane, 2016.
TOP RIGHT: On the set of an epic Sasol TVC with Schalk, Jean, Marius and Big Joe.
BOTTOM RIGHT: JP and Megan Pietersen's wedding.

ABOVE: Getting a photo with France striker Olivier Giroud at the ATP Finals in London, 2014.
TOP RIGHT: A Castle Lager TVC with Willie and Pieter-Steph in Joburg.
BOTTOM RIGHT: With the ladies in our number ones at the 2019 World Rugby Awards.

HSBC
ABOVE & BEYOND
WORLD RUGBY AWARDS
TUDOR
INTER NATIONAL RUGBY PLAYERS
LAND ROVER
Heineken

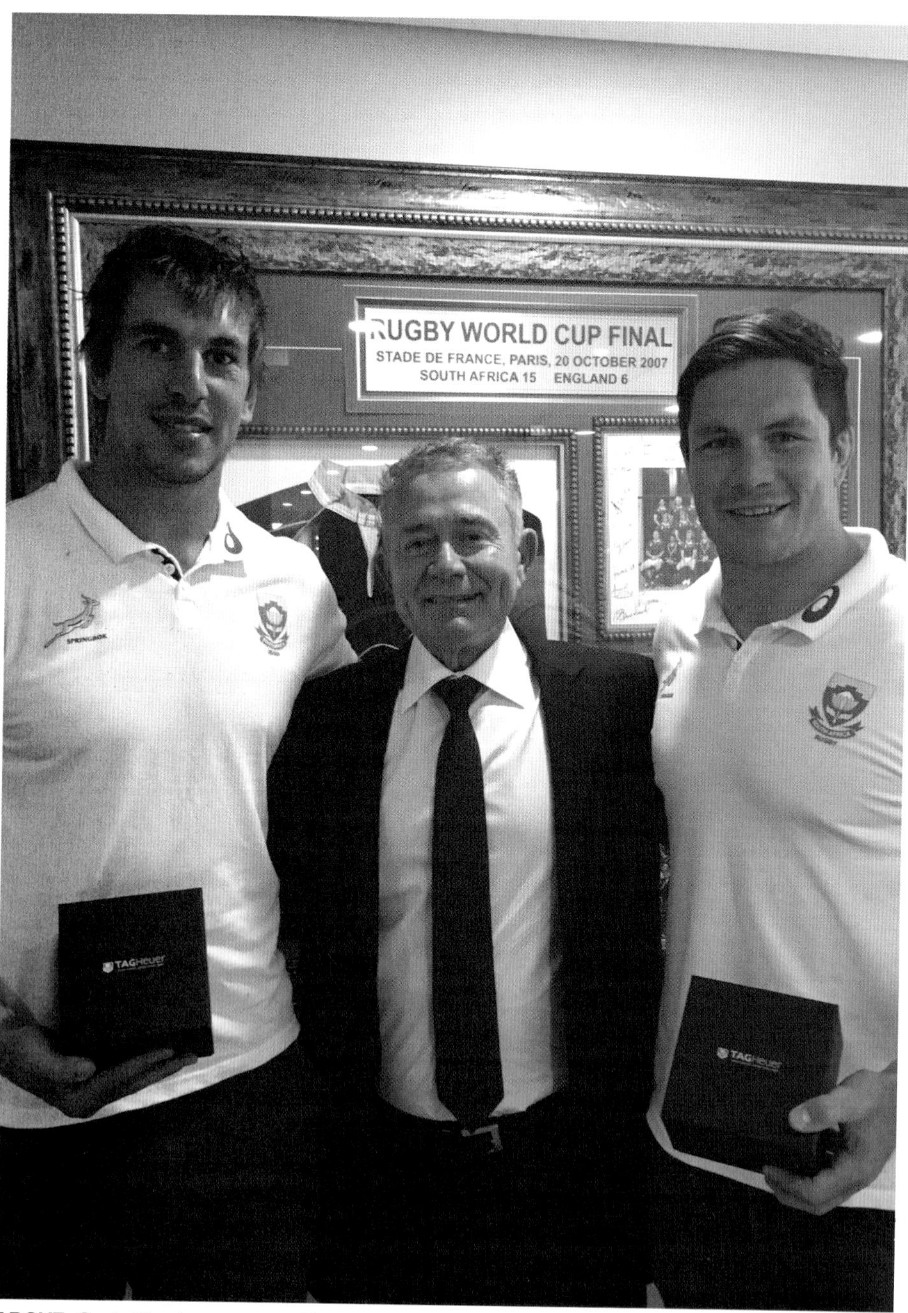

ABOVE: Gavin Varejes presents Eben and Flo with a watch to commemorate their 50th Tests.
TOP RIGHT: Ernie and Liezl at a post-match function in London, 2010.
BOTTOM RIGHT: Cameron van der Burgh handed out the Bok jerseys and let me hold his Olympic gold medal.

ABOVE: Sarah Louw at the 2020 Laureus World Sports Awards in Berlin.
TOP RIGHT: The Springboks won the Team of the Year award for the second time in Berlin.
BOTTOM RIGHT: Gavin Varejes and Tanya Harvey in Monaco, 2016.

Laureus
WORLD SPORTS
AWARDS
BERLIN 2020
Laureus
SPORT FOR
GOOD
IWC
MUFG
#LAURE

CELL C

ABOVE: Butch and Bismarck after winning the cricket match against the Proteas at the Wanderers in 2014.
TOP RIGHT: Meeting musician Bob Geldof at a function in Dublin.
BOTTOM RIGHT: With the guys at the 2015 World Rugby Awards in London.

TOP: With Rachel and Keziah Kolisi at the 2019 World Cup final in Yokohama.
ABOVE: A fun evening with three Bok legends and their wives.
TOP RIGHT: Siya takes a selfie with F1 star Lewis Hamilton at the 2020 Laureus Sports Awards.
BOTTOM RIGHT: A quick pic with Pat before he captained the Boks against the World XV at Wembley in 2016.

SPRINGBOKS

SPRINGBOK
BLUE LAB
TELECOM
SPRINGBOK

ABOVE: President Cyril Ramaphosa wishing Beast luck before the World Cup final.
TOP RIGHT: Daliah and I with actor Terry Crews, who popped in to say hi to the guys in the Loftus change room.
BOTTOM RIGHT: Celebrating in the change room with Beast, Bongi and Frans.

canterbury
ABSA

CHAMPIONS
JAPAN
JAPAN

ABOVE: Zelda was the SA flagbearer before a Nelson Mandela Challenge Plate match in PE.
TOP RIGHT: The Bok management at the Wanderers in 2014.
BOTTOM RIGHT: Drinks with Warren and Jesse.

MACSTEEL
MACSTEEL
MACSTEEL
MACSTEEL
HE BOKS INSPIRE
#PROTEAFIRE
ABSA

SPRINGBOK
SPRINGBOK

ABOVE: Showing John my World Cup medal after the final.
TOP RIGHT: My godchild Tyron Smit and his sister, Emma.
BOTTOM RIGHT: Zelda, Michele Burger and I in the stands at Twickenham.

TWICKENHAM

LEFT: On *Toks 'n Tjops* with Toks and Breytie.
BELOW (clockwise from top left): Ernie brought the famous Claret Jug to Twickenham to show the guys in 2012; meeting actor Bill Murray at the Laureus World Sports Awards in 2015; at a post-match function with John and Roxy Smit; One Direction drummer Josh Devine meeting Bryan at Gatwick Airport.
TOP RIGHT: Rene, Daliah and I at the ATP Finals in London.
BOTTOM RIGHT: Former France captain Fabian Galthié popped into the change room at the Stade de France.

TOP: Olympic gold medallist Wayde van Niekerk handed out the Bok jerseys in Bloemfontein.
ABOVE: At the MTN team farewell event for the 2019 World Cup with Motshidisi Mohono.
OPPOSITE PAGE: The famous flasks – empty!

ABOVE: Daliah and I taking in the sights of Venice on our off-day.
TOP RIGHT: Ahead of Pieter-Steph's 50th Test match in Shizuoka, 2019.
BOTTOM RIGHT: With All Blacks legend Richie McCaw.

SPRINGBOK
MTN
SPRINGBOK
MTN

ABOVE (clockwise): Princess Charlene of Monaco visited the Boks at Twickenham in 2016; Heinrich Brüssow's wife, Caroline, sang the national anthem before the 2017 Test in Bloem; Carla van der Merwe (Springboks office manager at SA Rugby) was a special guest of the Boks in Nelspruit.

OPPOSITE PAGE: A special moment with President Ramaphosa before the World Cup final.

SPRINGBOK
SPRINGBOK

ABOVE: Holding Bryan and a World Cup winner's medal for the second time.
RIGHT: The De Jager family soaking up the moment.

ABOVE: Visiting Old Trafford in Manchester with Daliah and the team, 2014.

Chapter 16

FEELING THE LOVE

It was early 2012 and I was on my way to Pilates when the phone rang. It was Heyneke Meyer, who had been appointed Springbok coach and successor to Peter de Villiers. Heyneke asked if I had a few minutes to chat about my experience of the Springboks and what I thought would be a 10-minute chat turned into two-and-a-half hours, with us discussing rugby, life skills and life philosophy. I had never interacted with Heyneke one-one-one and it soon became apparent that I was conducting a job interview-type phone call.

I had become accustomed to having my position questioned every time a new coach took over, but none had quite been as extensive in unpacking my role as this. I enjoyed the chat because he asked a lot of questions, which gave me the opportunity to give him insight into the portfolio and how I had evolved it since my introduction in 2001. Among the things he wanted to know was how I felt I could further grow the role, what value I felt I could add to his management team and he wanted to know about my previous experiences with the team and his coaching predecessors.

I felt very comfortable chatting to him and energised about the possibilities of the Springboks in the cycle between 2012 and 2015, and Heyneke came with a strong record after a decade at the Bulls, in which he had won the Currie Cup and Super Rugby.

The Bulls players in the Springboks had always spoken fondly of Heyneke and what was very apparent to me in that first phone call was his belief in tradition, discipline and the Springboks being ambassadors of the country. I've never known anyone in our management to sing our national anthem with such emotion and passion, and it didn't matter how many times I would line up next to Heyneke before a match, he always produced a stirring rendition of the anthem.

He was the exception to the other coaches when it came to the singing of the national anthem in that, where possible, he would be on the pitch, along with the on-field management, and lined up opposite the match-day squad. The other coaches all took up their positions in the coach's box before kick-off for the singing of the anthem.

Heyneke was very big on acknowledging milestones and achievements within the squad, rugby related or in a private capacity, and he always wanted there to be a celebration of these moments, be it a birthday, birth of a child or a Test record, and it's something we appreciated.

He liked to tell stories and the players told me that his pre-match speeches, directed exclusively at them and for their ears only, were legendary. The players always knew they were going to get something new at the team talk before every match.

He was also popular with the South African media and there was an obvious sense that they wanted Heyneke and the Springboks to be successful. He loved to tell the story about coal and how if you press it and press it and keep on working it, with dedication and purpose, it becomes a diamond.

Jake White had introduced the tradition of awarding a springbok skin after the match to the player of the day, as voted for by his teammates, and this was pretty special for the guy receiving it to be voted by his peers. To put it into perspective, Jean de Villiers received his first skin in his 88th Test, but Francois Louw got one in his first Test and quite a few thereafter.

The only time the skins ceremony was not held was after the 49-0 loss against the Wallabies in Brisbane, and the 57-0 loss against the All Blacks in Albany. I have those skins.

During Heyneke's term, the player who made the best tackle in a match was rewarded with a knife. It always seemed to go to Willem Alberts, aka the Bone Collector, for delivering the biggest hit.

The Springboks enjoyed a fantastic first two seasons under Heyneke and we lost just five times in 24 Tests in 2012 and 2013. The team was lauded internationally for the type of rugby they were playing and for the leadership of Heyneke, as coach, and Jean de Villiers as captain.

Heyneke, in 2014, was also the first Springbok coach to select Handré Pollard, when the flyhalf was still playing for the Junior Boks, and he made no secret of his belief in Handré's capability of becoming a World Cup winner and the best flyhalf in the world. It was well known to everyone that Heyneke had identified Handré as a teenage prospect when he was at Paarl Gymnasium in the Western Cape and had got an undertaking from the Pollard family that he would sign for the Bulls when leaving school. Heyneke believed in Handré in the same way Jake believed in Frans Steyn's potential when he first picked him as a 19-year-old to play for the Springboks in 2006. While Heyneke was convinced that Handré would be influential in the Springboks winning the 2015 World Cup, it was four years later than that, in Japan, that Handré guided the Springboks to the World Cup trophy.

Handré is a strong personality and leader within the squad and that rare breed of young player who can step into the Springboks environment and just belong there. Frans, despite being 19 when he joined the Springboks, was so confident in his ability, and Jaque Fourie was another youngster who never seemed fazed by being just 20 years old when he made his debut.

It would not surprise me to see Handré captain the Springboks in the next few years because he has always been a natural leader within the team and willingly taken on and embraced the responsibility of leadership. Despite being young enough to be my son, Handré was often a sounding board to me because he has such a wise head on his shoulders.

Heyneke, throughout his four-year tenure, was very loyal to those Bulls players who had succeeded for him at provincial and regional levels. From the moment he got the job Heyneke explored the possibility of Fourie du Preez making himself available for Test duty and Victor Matfield potentially coming out of retirement. At the time, Fourie was still playing for Eddie Jones' Suntory team in Japan, while Victor had quit rugby after the 2011 World Cup. Heyneke would get his wish in 2014 as Victor came out of retirement and Fourie made himself available for the Springboks. Both played an integral part in the 2015 World Cup and Fourie scored the match-winning try in the quarter-final against Wales at Twickenham.

Victor and Fourie were two of the biggest names in my 20 years with the Springboks; colossal on the field and their presence in the team room and change room was as big. Victor was there from the beginning with Harry Viljoen in 2001 and I watched him grow, mature and thrive as a Springbok.

Fourie was another player who commanded respect because of his ability and understated personality. He was one of those players who didn't have to tell you his worth in the team because his teammates and the opposition would be talking about his pedigree as a player. For Fourie, less was always more.

Heyneke was very thorough in everything he did and a student of rugby and life. He was always referencing a book, telling a tale and challenging mindsets and philosophies. His management style was details-driven and there was consistent follow-through from team manager Ian Schwartz, which made for a very professional management environment.

I got the necessary support from Heyneke to do my job and this was always the case for me, regardless of who was coaching the Springboks in my tenure, because no matter their management style, they all treated me with the respect they treated any male member of the management. This carried through to the female members of the management team over the years.

People may expect that, because rugby is seen as a male-dominated sporting environment, my long journey with the Springboks must be littered with challenges related to bias and prejudice. But the truth is that, under all the coaches I worked with between 2000 and 2020, this perception remained just that – a perception – and I found that hard work, regardless of gender, was recognised and respected. I was also always backed by SA Rugby CEO Rian Oberholzer, in the early part of my career, and Jurie Roux in the latter.

One of the most special nights of my career highlighted the inclusive nature of the extended rugby community and the manner in which my 150th Test was celebrated.

I was always involved with the organisation of a player's first-Test capping ceremony. Where possible, we'd ensure that the player's family was present for the official awarding of that prized first Test cap, which could be challenging because it wasn't always in a structured context. For example, Herschel Jantjies, after making his Bok debut against the Wallabies at Ellis Park in 2019, had to be rushed to the airport to get on a plane to New Zealand for a Test against the All Blacks. We had to hold his capping ceremony in the change room and the adrenaline was flowing as we tried to get his family inside to share this incredible career milestone, and then get him to the airport and on the plane.

It was moments like these, when I saw what it meant to the player and their family, which made everything seem worthwhile. I have always believed that needing to do something is very different to wanting to do something. When it came to the players, I wanted to take care of as much as possible for them off the field, so that their only focus would be on-field. I did so because I wanted to do it and not because anyone had an expectation that it should be done for them.

The players would joke about my black book having every contact around the world and they would say if anyone could make a phone call to anyone it was me, but a lot of those phone calls were made possible because of the pulling power of the Springboks. I had built up an extensive global network after 20 years of being with the team, and the appeal of the Springboks as a brand never waned, no matter who the contact or who they represented. This was a point I would often reiterate to the players and coaches when it came to interacting with sponsors, investors in the game, the media and most importantly the supporters.

I insisted that, where possible, every last autograph got signed and that everyone's request for a photo was accommodated. My stock phrase to the players was to make that last autograph because it is a very different situation when no one wants your autograph anymore.

Win or lose, signing memorabilia after a match was a non-negotiable for the players because the Springbok supporters wanted that player autograph regardless of the result. There was always a youngster waiting to meet his or her hero and that hero's behaviour was going to shape this kid's idea of the Springboks.

The longer I was a part of the management, the stronger my voice when it came to the bond between players, sponsors and supporters, and there was certainly a greater appreciation for that relationship in 2019 than there had been in 2000.

The younger Annelee was a bit more hot-headed than I am today, but I learned my lessons along the way and I got taught a few too. Tsogo Sun's Hazel Lewis, in the early 2000s, said to me: 'There is no need to be rude, Annelee.' It was such a powerful jolt because being at the top of my profession within the team had made me arrogant, even if I wasn't consciously aware of it.

Hazel, whose warm personality defined the kind of relationship that has always prospered with Tsogo Sun and the Springboks, gave me a big wake-up call in that there were different ways of asking for things and getting the right results. I was humbled by my early interaction with Hazel and, as an anchor, I always took myself back to that moment. She remains a dear friend.

Another experience that provided perspective was witnessing how the players responded whenever we remembered their personal milestones.

Heyneke's belief in celebrating every type of victory was consistent with my outlook and, to me, a birthday was a victory so there had to be a cake and a sense of belonging because that player was away from his family on this special day. It may seem small, but making a fuss of a player on his birthday never got small within the squad.

Getting to 50 Test caps in the earlier years was a milestone that few had achieved, and in 2001 in Auckland, I proposed to coach Harry Viljoen that something special be stitched into the Test jersey of Mark Andrews and Joost van der Westhuizen to acknowledge their record-breaking 75th Tests, and he thought it was a great idea.

I loved the reaction of Mark and Joost when they saw the jerseys celebrating their record achievement. This has now become a Bok tradition as the match details are embroidered on every Test jersey.

It would be the same when Percy Montgomery became the first Springbok Test centurion. What made it even more memorable was that Monty got to play his 100th Test at Newlands in Cape Town, where he had first played for Western Province and the Stormers, and which was also a few hundred metres away from where he had been schooled, at SACS.

Monty's 100th was a milestone that broke a barrier for the Springboks because he showed it could be done and five other players have since played 100-plus Tests. We made a big fuss about Monty, even though he wanted to treat the Test just like any other. The Springbok Test cap has always been green, other than the green cap with gold trim which is used to mark a player's 50th Test, but it was decided that the 100th Test cap would be gold.

Monty had no idea that we had arranged an on-field 100th Test capping ceremony for him, with the president of SA Rugby, Oregan Hoskins, presenting him with the first-ever gold Springbok Test cap.

On the day before the Test, after the official team photo was taken, we as a squad had also arranged for a unique Bok team photo with every player wearing a blonde wig to commemorate the moment with Monty. It was a very fun moment but also one that spoke to the admiration there was from his teammates.

The coaches, throughout my time, would often single out an extraordinary player achievement, be it a Test record, a goal-kicking record or a try-scoring record. The players usually were quite shy, but I know it meant a lot to them to be acknowledged by their peers.

Bryan Habana's try-scoring moment against Namibia at the 2011 World Cup was another of those unforgettable celebrations because he had become the Springboks' all-time leading try-scorer and each time there was a moment to savour within the squad, it would be a celebration.

I was always mindful of every Test I was privileged to be a part of and one day, in conversation with Lynn Naudé, Absa's head of sponsorship and events, she asked how long I had been with the Springboks. I mentioned that I was approaching 150 Tests and thought nothing more about our conversation.

Lynn is an inspiration to me in what she has achieved in the sports industry and how she has always owned her space and backed herself to get the job done. I got to know her well when Absa was the lead sponsor of the Boks and I learned a lot through our interactions.

She was also a driving force in the quality of the relationship and the strength of the partnership between Absa and the Springboks. Lynn was very generous in wanting to add value to the sponsorship because she always spoke of the alignment of the two brands and the iconic nature of the two being such strong South African legacy brands. It really was a proudly South African relationship.

Lynn had worked for the International Cricket Council which was based in Monaco and for Visa on the 2010 Fifa World Cup. She was ahead of her time professionally and is a leader in sports sponsorships. I have a high regard and respect for Lynn and often bounce ideas off her.

I had no idea that she had remembered our conversation and had set in motion the most extravagant of nights for me.

I am usually on top of everything and in most cases aware of what is going on when it comes to surprise parties and the arranging of special occasions. I would think that I recognise the signs because I have been so integral to the planning of victory celebrations, but when it came to my own, I didn't have a clue of how much was being done for me.

The celebration of my 100th Test had been very intimate, spent with my folks and a few friends, while Charles Wessels had commissioned Richie Ryall, the former Western Province cricketer and renowned South African artist, to paint a portrait of me that chronicled every Test match. But the party in Cape Town for my 150th Test was a big affair, as I would find out to my great surprise on the Thursday evening before the Saturday Test.

My focus was always that I wanted the players to get the recognition and that was very much the view of all the management. The Springboks are about the players and their performances and achievements, and working with them was enough reward and recognition for me. It never occurred to me that anyone would put in the same amount of thought and effort for me.

I was so wrong. Charles and Lynn, with the support of Heyneke and all the sponsors I'd worked with, arranged a 150th Test surprise party for me. Charles had asked me to keep the Thursday night schedule open, under the pretext of having dinner with a new sponsor and Andy Marinos, who was SA Rugby's commercial head at the time (he is now Rugby Australia's CEO).

I thought it a bit odd, given it was in a Test week, but as we were in Cape Town, where I live, I didn't give it too much thought as I had spent the evenings between the hotel and my home.

Unbeknown to me, my parents, brother, sister-in-law, niece and nephew were flown to Cape Town by SA Rugby, accommodated by Tsogo Sun and given tickets to the Test match as part of the celebration.

SA Rugby and Absa also combined to fly in John Smit and Victor Matfield, two of the longest serving Springboks during my time. Monty and Breyton Paulse, who were based in Cape Town, were also invited, as was the rest of the team management. Because it was on the Thursday night of a Test week, only the captain, Jean de Villiers, was given permission to attend, and Schalk Burger and Bryan Habana were especially disappointed to have missed out.

Roxy Smit and Michele Burger, with whom I have always had a close relationship, were also there along with SAB's Rob Fleming, Guy Kilfoil from BMW and Neil Fraser and Hazel from Tsogo Sun, among other sponsors.

None of this was known to me and, after commercial obligations in the morning, I had spent the afternoon at home and was back at the team hotel, The Cullinan, on Thursday early evening to meet Charles for this phantom sponsor dinner.

I left my room and as I was walking towards the lifts to go down and meet Charles, my friend and colleague Daliah Hurwitz came out of the lift dressed in the team number twos, which was a grey suit. I was taken aback and asked why she was formally dressed. She mumbled something about a medical dinner and disappeared down the corridor. Immediately I sensed something was up and hated not knowing, as I always knew everything that was going on.

Charles and I took a quick drive to the Cape Quarter retail centre and he was particularly vague about who we were having dinner with and spent the time focusing on the Test week activities and operationally what had to happen on the Friday. It was all a bit odd to me but I'd often attended rugby dinners or meetings where I wasn't necessarily briefed on the details, so again didn't overly think about this dinner.

I went up the escalator, chatting away to Charles and when we got to the top, I looked directly into the restaurant, and the first people I saw were my parents, and my niece and nephew, Izy and Max. Everyone shouted, 'Surprise!', and my goodness it was a surprise!

The entire team management was there in formal dress, with only Charles and I not in team attire because it was the only way he could keep it a surprise from me.

SuperSport commentator Matthew Pearce greeted everyone on my behalf and asked my dad to speak. He was just too overwhelmed and emotional, and, like me, he never enjoyed being behind a microphone.

My brother said a few words and John spoke, and then I had no choice but to speak. My unprepared speech was just one big thank you to the players, management, sponsors, and friends who were there, but mostly to my parents, who had sparked my love for the Springboks when we watched them beat the British & Irish Lions in the rain at Boet Erasmus Stadium in 1980.

It was such a happy evening and an incredible feeling to be appreciated and celebrated, and the next day the players all individually came to congratulate me. I felt honoured and blessed to be a part of the Springbok family and I felt the love.

Eben Etzebeth – Bok captain

There are so many special memories of Annelee Murray that it's hard to choose just one, so I have decided to write a few things that we as Springboks are thankful for:

You were our go-to person for any issues we had, both on and off the field. No matter what, your door was always open.

You always made us feel extra special on our birthdays and made sure we felt at home even when we were miles away on tour.

You always had our back and were the kindest to us, but ruthless to anyone who meant us harm.

You always went that extra mile to organise everything for our partners and family members, and treated them as if they were your own.

You were one of the most important members of the Springbok squad, although you never wanted any credit for it.

AL, there are so many things to be thankful for.

You are an irreplaceable part of the squad and will forever be remembered as the mother of the Springboks.

Thank you for everything. You will be missed.

WE LOVE YOU!

Chapter 17

#StrongerTogether

The main focus for the team is rugby, so I always had to ensure that the sponsorship obligations were met with minimal intrusion, but no less care. Where possible, we would try to do all of the television commercials (TVCs) during the Super Rugby season, so that by the time the Boks came into camp, the off-field promotional aspects were done.

I always knew the value of TVCs aligned to Springbok rugby, but over the years I got an even greater appreciation for the power of these emotive commercials and the significance of strong sponsorships and investments into the game.

A lot of my time in the pre-international season period, the months between January and May, would be spent working closely with sponsors and the players. I was always grateful to the various provincial unions and regional franchises for how they accommodated the requests when players were needed for a Springbok activity. Over the years, it was also made easier because my relationships got stronger with the provinces and I had insight into their working weeks, which allowed me to be more effective in scheduling these shoots.

A lot of my friends would casually ask me what it is exactly that I do with the team. It was never meant to offend because their exposure to the team and knowledge of the team so often was the 80 minutes of the Test match.

A big part of what I did in the build-up to the Test season involved managing the relationship between the squad, the sponsors and the South African rugby broadcaster SuperSport, by educating players and coaches about the sponsors' contractual rights and the difference between a team sponsor, event sponsor and supplier sponsor. I would manage those expectations and, within the Springbok context, it was my job to make sure all contractual obligations were met.

There was a lot of work done in that pre-international season period because you can't film a television commercial, as one example, when the team is together and playing Test matches.

I worked closely with MyPlayers – which represents South Africa's professional rugby players and manages their image rights – and the sponsors were educated as to the dos and don'ts when it came to players and their brand promotion.

The Springboks is a collective and there can never be only one person in an aligned campaign and all promotional advertisements with Springbok sponsors featured three or more players.

Some sponsors would request certain players as a preference and, where possible, we would assist. Outside of the Test windows, we used players during their off-days to fulfil obligations and sometimes this was hard to juggle because the provincial unions didn't always have the same off-days.

During the international season it is quite basic when it comes to off-field player commitments and it may involve a function, signing session or visit to the corporate's headquarters. But the out-of-season TVCs could be lengthy and time consuming, and the challenge was to keep the players interested and motivated throughout the day.

Players are athletes not actors, even though some were more comfortable than others in front of the camera. The players, with each year, became more accustomed to this being part of their job and they experienced the value associated with these powerful sponsor-related marketing campaigns.

I would often sit in on creative meetings with the sponsor's advertising and marketing creative teams to provide input about the characters within the squad and give context to the personalities of the players. Once the storyline was confirmed, which had to be signed off by SA Rugby, there were many technical aspects and moving parts to the shoots, with awareness around opposition sponsor logos, stadium names, all types of other logos, the ball and anything that could be interpreted as a breach of the contract. I was well versed on these contracts to make sure the Springboks were protected and met their obligations.

The sponsors were a pleasure to work with but the challenge would often be in working with the many different creative teams on the shoots, defining the boundaries of what was a must-have and what constituted a nice-to-have.

Though I was committed to deliver the desired result for the agencies, my priority was the players. If the shoot was scheduled for three hours, then I made sure that was a hard deadline and the players left on time.

With each passing year, this process became more streamlined and easier to manage as I came to grips with balancing expectations against the reality of using athletes as actors. Technology in the past few years has made the process easier and more comfortable, but the demands in the planning remained the same.

The World Cup years were always more intense and very different because of the embargoes, the restrictions and how each World Cup came with its own set of challenges related to sponsors who exclusively sponsored the tournament. The 2009 British & Irish Lions series was also unique in the intensity that it brought to the annual schedule and also the creative brilliance in promoting the Springboks and the three Tests against the Lions.

The 2009 Boks'TVC for the Lions series was one of my favourites but also one of the more demanding on the players, in terms of time and location, because it was on top of Table Mountain and it involved them standing on the edge of a rock, which didn't help my nerves. It was one of those shoots where I could have done with my match-day flask!

For the most part, the producers and directors were good to work with, and my standard word of advice to them was to make the most of the first hour as that was usually when the players were at their most emotive.

Players aren't complicated individuals when it comes to most things and on shoot days, they wanted to be well fed and briefed on their role. The sponsors would always try to create a filming environment that provided a comfortable experience because the happier the player, the better the performance.

Not every shoot goes as planned and sometimes it is the unplanned that becomes the most powerful of finished products. For example, the #StrongerTogether campaign before the 2019 World Cup, which shows Siya Kolisi singing the anthem with his son, Nic, on the phone, was never planned. Siya and his son love singing the national anthem and he took a call from Nic just before the shoot was about to start. Nic had asked him if he was with the Springboks, Siya said yes and, spontaneously, father and son started to sing the national anthem. A cameraman just happened to be close by, testing the sound and visuals, and he recorded the telephonic interaction between Siya and Nic. It became such an emotive part of the actual campaign advertisement.

I loved the #StrongerTogether campaign because it spoke to the personality of the squad and the inclusiveness of the families and a nation.

They knew they were never alone and knew just how much stronger they felt having their families close and the support of their friends and the passionate Bok supporters. It was a common thread, because of this belief, that the Springboks were stronger together. They were not just 15 players on the field, they were backed by a nation.

The #StrongerTogether campaign was filmed over several weeks and had so many beautiful moments, and it reminded me so much of the 2003 'Our Blood is Green' campaign because it spoke to all South Africans.

A very special campaign was the Sasol one we filmed in Elgin, in the Western Cape, where they recreated a village scene from more than 100 years ago to tell the story of William Webb Ellis and the birth of rugby. They put a unique twist to it, which involved opposite sides of the village playing each other in a game that began with somebody picking up a ball and running with it.

John Smit, Schalk Burger, Brent Russell and Jean de Villiers featured prominently in that advert. It was one of the more demanding shoots and probably the biggest on-set production over my 20 years. I loved being part of that shoot because there were so many extras and so much detail to the advertisement and the players were also dressed in outfits appropriate to the period.

The MTN, FNB, Sasol and SA Breweries TVCs were always very popular. And SuperSport were exceptional in the quality of their emotive campaigns and the quick turnaround time – they took just two hours to shoot one campaign that featured the players speaking on what the jersey means to them. I worked closely with Thato Monale, SuperSport's head of rugby production, and so passionate was Thato about the game that it was not uncommon for him to call me late at night with a new idea that he wanted to shoot the next day!

Absa's 2012 #HumanSpirit campaign was very good because it highlighted that there is no team in the world like the Springboks and no supporters like Springbok supporters. South Africa's love for rugby is different to anything I have experienced throughout the world.

The environment in professional rugby has changed so much since 2000. The modern player's awareness and appreciation for what it takes to be a professional athlete is on a different level, and they take the same selfless work ethic into promoting the brand as they do when they run onto the field in a Test match.

The players are very big on supporting the Blitzboks, as they are with all of South Africa's leading athletes and teams. There is a lot of interest in the Proteas and Bafana's performances, and more recently the netballers and hockey teams. The squad was also very interested in the successes of South African athletes, swimmers, golfers and tennis players. Players were regularly in contact with other sportspeople and shared any South African success and celebrated it with a similar pride as they would any of their own rugby successes.

We were together when the 2016 Olympics were on. We watched the Blitzboks in Rio and when Wayde van Niekerk won Olympic gold, the team room erupted in celebration.

The networking and close relationships formed over time also allowed us to engage with cricket and soccer, and it led to the establishment of the Springboks versus Proteas cricket match, which was first played in 2013 and then 2014 and 2017 in Cape Town and Johannesburg. The matches were well supported and it was only a scheduling issue that prevented the exhibition continuing in 2018 and 2019, while the Covid pandemic has put a hold on something that was so popular among the two teams and South African sports fans.

We tried to arrange a similar type of cross-code match with Bafana but the soccer schedules were so packed and so many of the players are based overseas that logistically we just couldn't find a solution to make it happen.

Castle Lager is synonymous with South African sport and it was exciting to be involved with a Castle advertisement that combined the Springboks, Proteas and Bafana. For the first time it included support staff like physiotherapists and backroom staff, which only added to the bond that the Springboks shared with these national teams.

The cricket matches between the Boks and Proteas were fun and Mark Jury of SuperSport was supportive of everything both myself and Lerato Malekutu (formerly with the Proteas management) suggested and requested.

The inaugural Nelson Mandela Legacy Cup match at Newlands will always be closest to my heart because it was the first one. Former Proteas captain Graeme Smith was our manager and current Proteas coach Mark Boucher coached the Springboks.

We also involved ex-players and always had the luxury that most of the players had played cricket at school and some had been very good cricketers before choosing rugby as their profession. The first-choice wicketkeeper,

Butch James, was a popular choice as were Tiaan Liebenberg, Victor Matfield and Willem Alberts.

The Proteas won the first and third match as Victor's innings at the Wanderers helped the Boks win the second. The players loved it and I know it is something they want revived.

These matches were always followed by an informal post-match get-together, when the two squads combined for a laugh, reminisced and handed out fines. A few Castles were downed and for those who did not drink alcohol, a cold drink.

A particularly fond memory of the series is of Trevor Nyakane, by now famous for his dance moves, coming out to bat. The burly prop strode to the middle of the pitch in a face-off with Proteas bowler Mangaliso Mosehle. There was an awkward pause before the two of them got their shoulders rolling in a back-pedalling dance to their respective ends of the pitch.

Pieter-Steph du Toit – Bok captain

Annelee was with the Boks for 20 years. When I got my first cap, she was already an established pillar of strength in the Springbok setup.

When getting to know her, I soon realised that when you ask Annelee for something, you can consider it done. She is efficient and excellent in her work, a part of the family, the head girl and mom of the Boks. Annelee was always available to us.

She is the one who organised everything for our wives when we needed to focus on our games. When you need anything as a player, you will phone her and she will sort it out. Even when you are injured on the field, she takes charge and phones your wife to let her know everything is under control and comforts her.

You could always count on Annelee. She is loving, caring, supportive and extraordinary.

Nothing was ever too much trouble for Annelee in the eight years we worked together and it has been an absolute pleasure.

I was sad to see you go, but I wish you a wonderful time ahead and I hope that you will enjoy your new venture.

Thank you for creating a better world for all of us!

Chapter 18

A TOUR TO END ALL TOURS

I once bowed to a woman. She was the Queen of England and I wasn't meant to bow, but to curtsey. The Springboks were in London and I was invited to a function that the Queen would be attending. I was briefed that there was a possibility I would meet the Queen, and the protocol was for men to bow and women to curtsy. I duly rehearsed my curtsy but when it came time to meet Her Majesty, the protocols vanished from my mind and, inexplicably, I bowed.

It's a memory I shared with Fourie du Preez in 2015 when he, as the Bok captain, joined other World Cup team representatives on a visit to Buckingham Palace. We had a good laugh and I warned him not to curtsy!

Talking of a majestic lady, the women I got to work with during my time at the Springboks are the type you'd acknowledge with a bow because, professionally, they are among the best in the world and, as individuals, they are just such good people.

Physiotherapist Rene Naylor joined the Springboks in 2008 and is still with the team. I have such respect and admiration for her professionally and as a mother, given that for the past decade she has juggled being on tour with raising the most delightful son, Cullin. In the earliest days of motherhood, she often had her son in camp, yet somehow managed to remain this great mother while also do this amazing job as one of the team's physiotherapists.

Ren is a strong-willed personality and very confident and we didn't initially gel when she joined the Springboks. She and I are both strong-willed and it took us some time to get on the same page and complement each other in our roles. We remain good friends today.

Ren started her rugby journey with Silvertree RFC in Mitchell's Plain before moving to the Western Province U19 team and later the Stormers. She then joined the Boks in 2008.

Ren took a break from the Springboks after the 2015 World Cup to spend more time at home with her son and focus on her own physiotherapy practices. She returned in 2018 and it was so great having her for the 2019 World Cup campaign.

Dr Tanushree Pillay has spent the past 15 years working with some of the best teams and athletes in the world as a physiotherapist. She has a doctorate and is such a professional and wonderful human being. Her personality brought warmth to the management team and her experience of working with Team South Africa at the Commonwealth Games and the 2012 Olympics in London added great value.

Zeenat Simjee's appointment to the management in 2019 was very significant because she is the Springboks' first full-time dietician. There have always been dietician consultants to the team and they would move in and out during pre-season and alignment camps but were never a permanent fixture. Zee's role was integral to the Bok conditioning plan and seeing her grow in this role was inspirational.

Daliah Hurwitz joined the Boks in 2009 as the team's first full-time masseuse and, in eight years, proved to be a key cog in the team's medical evolution. Dals has gone on to work with Munster, Super Rugby teams, the Proteas cricket team and more recently the USA Eagles. She remains my travel buddy and we'd often extend our stay after a tour to eat and drink our way around Europe and recharge our batteries.

Zeenat, Rene and Tanu were all at the 2019 World Cup and Dals, who had left the Springboks to expand her private practice as a sports massage specialist, also left an indelible mark on the squad during her 101 Tests.

I have been privileged to work with such incredibly strong, gifted and influential ladies in the Springboks. It is a credit to the respective Bok coaches that they have always been willing to appoint the best, like Jake did with Sherylle Calder in 2007, regardless of gender. I do consider the Springboks the pioneers in world rugby when it comes to breaking down gender barriers, even though it never felt like any of the appointments were a conscious effort to do so, but rather an acknowledgement that all of the ladies in the Springboks were there because we were considered the best.

Fran Leighton is another professional lady I met in 2013 when she was a liaison working for World Rugby. Fran was a great resource in advising me as we planned for the 2015 Rugby World Cup, she later joined the England's RFU, and it was a very special moment for me after the 2019

World Cup final to have a drink with Frankie in the Bok change room.

Chelsea Jones, whose portfolio with the Australian team was similar to mine, is another remarkable young woman. She was 13 years old when I met her at the 2007 World Cup. She was in Paris with her dad, Eddie, who at the time was serving as a specialist coach to the Springboks.

Chelsea was very interested in what I was doing and said that it was something she was inspired to do. It's very satisfying to know I played a part in her career choice.

I have mentioned the women who have really left their mark, be it in the team, among the opposition and with the sponsors, but the biggest thank you is to those women within the squad for being so good at their jobs and having such an influence in the success of the Springboks in my journey that lasted 20 years.

When I think of Springbok journeys, it isn't mine that comes to mind first, but the story of the 1937 Springboks to Australia and New Zealand, and the sacrifices made to complete a trip that would last nearly half the year.

I had heard the story told and shared my experience with Rassie Erasmus, prior to the squad leaving for Japan. He wasn't initially convinced that the players would relate to something from 1937, despite it being the only time the Springboks had won a Test series in New Zealand. Rassie's initial hesitation was simply down to the psyche of the modern player and his ability to sit through an hour history lesson, even though it spoke to the core values of who they were and what they represented.

It wasn't so much the Test series win that I was focusing on, but the sacrifice these men made for the Springbok jersey – the time they were away from their families, the boat travel from South Africa to Australia and New Zealand, and the travelling within Australia, from the west to the east, and in New Zealand from the North Island to the South Island and vice-versa. The 1937 Springboks, with something like 29 players and two management, played five Tests (two wins against Australia and two wins from three against the All Blacks) and 29 tour matches in total. They lost only the first Test to the All Blacks and one tour game to New South Wales in Sydney. They travelled by boat, which was one month there and one month back, and were on tour for a further four months. They were away from home for half the year.

A lot was being made of teams having to be in Japan for nine weeks at the 2019 World Cup and I felt the story of the 1937 Springboks gave context to what those before us had given up to become world champions of rugby.

Rassie, who was always open to a discussion and a debate, and prepared to listen and be supportive if he felt it was going to benefit the players, agreed to have Michael Charton, a wonderful storyteller, come and tell the story of Springbok rugby's first unofficial world champions.

The players loved the session and it proved very inspiring. I was pleased because again I felt I had added that little extra that Clive Woodward had spoken about back in 2004 when challenging the management to always look for marginal gains that may give the player a mental or physical edge.

That night was very special for the 2019 World Cup squad because it made nine weeks, flying and living in comfort with all the first-world trappings, seem very comfortable when compared to the 1937 Springboks.

The rugby was never going to be as comfortable, but it wouldn't be a World Cup if it was easy. From the moment we arrived in Japan to when we left, the squad united to do justice to every player who had ever worn the Springbok jersey.

Those nine weeks in Japan encapsulated everything that is good about the Springboks. The five days spent travelling South Africa in November 2019, thanking the millions who had supported our every move, was an ending to my time with the Boks that I could never have scripted or even imagined.

I am privileged to have experienced the Springboks and every one of those 248 players who came through the team room over 20 years will always have a special place in my heart.

Duane Vermeulen – Bok captain

When I hear the name Annelee Murray, the first things that jump to mind are: strong woman, dedication, passion, leader and the best in the industry, and all of the above she most definitely is.

But if you are a player, or the partner of a player, she is much more. Mama Annelee, the glue that kept everything and everyone together, the shoulder to cry on, the friend who listens, the adviser, the rock, and most of all the most inspirational person you will ever meet. As a player, she takes you under her wing, guides you, helps you and makes sure you get the best treatment.

She is the go-to person for EVERYTHING! She will go out of her way to make sure you are settled in and know what is expected of you.

But when you walk into the hotel, stadium or get onto a bus as the wife, girlfriend or partner of one of the players, you really get to know this amazing woman. I think she is the definition of a SUPERWOMAN!

Annelee is the friendly face that greets you for the first time, already knowing your name and surname, and where you are from. It's as if she's known you for a lifetime.

Annelee took such special care of the details to make sure everything was always a breeze and comfortable, going the extra mile to see to everyone's needs (from prams to carriers, food, drinks, accommodation ... the list is endless) and make sure that everything ran on time, and not a second too late!

But most of all, Annelee was there in the highs, the lows, and all the in-betweens.

If a player went down with an injury, Annelee would be on the phone with his wife, girlfriend or partner within five minutes to give an update.

She will be dearly missed in the game. The boots that need to be filled are like a pair of size 15 rugby boots – MASSIVE!

WE SALUTE YOU, ANNELEE!

SPRINGBOKS' RECORD DURING ANNELEE'S TENURE

A total of 235 Tests and nine tour matches were played by the Springboks between 16 June 2001 and the 2019 World Cup final on 2 November.

Of the 235 Test matches, 143 were won, 85 lost and seven drawn for a win percentage of 60.85.

Of the nine tour games, four were won, four lost and one drawn, for a win percentage of 44.44.

On the following pages, Bok captains are indicated with number of Tests in brackets. Five captains (Joost van der Westhuizen, Rassie Erasmus, Bob Skinstad, Corné Krige and André Vos) also captained in Test matches before 2001.

A total of 17 players were used as captains during this period, while Juan Smith and Pat Lambie also captained one tour game each.

COMPLETE LIST OF SPRINGBOKS FROM 2001-2019

Joost van der Westhuizen [89]
(3 Tests as captain – 10 Tests overall)
Ollie le Roux [54]
Mark Andrews [77]
James Dalton [43]
Japie Mulder [34]
Os du Randt [80]
Toks van der Linde [7]
Johan Ackermann [13]
André Venter [66]
André Snyman [38]
Breyton Paulse [64]
Rassie Erasmus [36]
(1 Test as captain overall)
Percy Montgomery [102]
Pieter Rossouw [43]
Bob Skinstad [42]
(4 Tests and 1 tour game as captain – 12 Tests overall)
Thinus Delport [18]
Willie Meyer [26]
Dale Santon [4]
Gaffie du Toit [14]
Stefan Terblanche [37]
Robbie Kempson [37]
Selborne Boome [20]
Braam van Straaten [21]
Robbie Fleck [31]
Deon Kayser [13]
Corné Krige [39]
(17 Tests as captain – 18 Tests overall)
André Vos [33]
(3 Tests as captain – 16 Tests overall)
Cobus Visagie [29]
Albert van den Berg [51]
Wayne Julies [11]
De Wet Barry [39]
John Smit [111]
(83 Tests and 3 tour games as captain)
Louis Koen [15]
Jannes Labuschagne [11]
AJ Venter [25]
Jaco van der Westhuyzen [32]
Ricardo Loubscher [4]
Craig Davidson [5]
Delarey du Preez [2]
Lawrence Sephaka [24]
Hottie Louw [3]
Victor Matfield [127]
(23 Tests and 2 tour games as captain)

Quinton Davids [9]
Hendrik Gerber [2]
Etienne Fynn [2]
Marius Joubert [30]
Dean Hall [13]
Butch James [42]
Conrad Jantjes [24]
Neil de Kock [10]
Lukas van Biljon [13]
Joe van Niekerk [52]
Trevor Halstead [6]
Adrian Jacobs [34]
Deon de Kock [2]
André Pretorius [31]
Bolla Conradie [18]
Warren Britz [1]
Daan Human [4]
Brent Russell [23]
Faan Rautenbach [14]
Werner Greeff [11]
Danie Coetzee [15]
Shaun Sowerby [1]
Hendro Scholtz [5]
Bakkies Botha [85]
Deon Carstens [9]
Jean de Villiers [109]
(37 Tests as captain)
Friedrich Lombard [2]
Wessel Roux [3]
Pierre Uys [1]
Pedrie Wannenburg [20]
Marco Wentzel [2]
CJ van der Linde [75]
Norman Jordaan [1]
Ashwin Willemse [19]
Wikus van Heerden [14]
Richard Bands [11]
Juan Smith [70]
(1 tour game as captain)
Gcobani Bobo [6]
Jorrie Müller [6]
Gus Theron [0]*
**Theron was selected as a Springbok for the away leg of the 2003 Tri-Nations tournament. He was due to make his Springbok debut against Australia, but due to a hamstring injury he had to withdraw from the game. He was never again selected for the Springboks.*
Geo Cronjé [3]
Chris Bezuidenhout [4]
Jaque Fourie [72]
Derick Hougaard [8]
Schalk Burger [86]
(1 Test as captain)
Danie Rossouw [63]
Henno Mentz [2]
Fourie du Preez [76]
(4 Tests as captain)
Jacques Cronjé [32]
Eddie Andrews [23]
Gerrie Britz [13]
Hanyani Shimange [9]
Tim Dlulane [1]
Solly Tyibilika [8]
Gurthrö Steenkamp [53]
Michael Claassens [8]
Bryan Habana [124]
Jongi Nokwe [4]
Tonderai Chavhanga [4]
Ricky Januarie [47]
Gary Botha [12]
Meyer Bosman [3]

Wynand Olivier [38]
Johann Muller [24]
(1 Test and 1 tour game as captain)
Akona Ndungane [11]
JP Pietersen [70]
Chiliboy Ralepelle [25]
Pierre Spies [53]
BJ Botha [25]
Ruan Pienaar [88]
Bevan Fortuin [2]
Hilton Lobberts [2]
Jaco Pretorius [2]
Francois Steyn [67]
Kabamba Floors [1]
Waylon Murray [3]
Luke Watson [10]
Bismarck du Plessis [79]
Jannie du Plessis [70]
Peter Grant [5]
Heinke van der Merwe [5]
Ryan Kankowski [20]
Wian du Preez [1]
Barend Pieterse [0]
(1 tour game)
Tiaan Liebenberg [5]
Andries Bekker [29]
Brian Mujati [12]
Beast Mtawarira [117]
Odwa Ndungane [9]
Schalk Brits [15]
(2 Tests as captain)
Adriaan Strauss [66]
(12 Tests as captain)
Heinrich Brüssow [23]
Earl Rose [0]
(2 Tour games)
Morné Steyn [66]
Zane Kirchner [31]
Heini Adams [0]
(2 tour games)
Juan de Jongh [19]
Francois Hougaard [46]
Riaan Viljoen [0]
(2 tour games)
Alistair Hargreaves [4]
Ashley Johnson [3]
Bandise Maku [1]
Dewald Potgieter [6]
Davon Raubenheimer [0]
(2 tour games)
Jean Deysel [4]
Francois Louw [76]
Gio Aplon [17]
Bjorn Basson [11]
Flip van der Merwe [37]
Elton Jantjies [37]
Patrick Lambie [56]
(1 tour game as captain)
Lwazi Mvovo [17]
Willem Alberts [43]
Keegan Daniel [5]
Coenie Oosthuizen [30]
Deon Stegmann [6]
Charl McLeod [1]
Andries Strauss [0]
(1 tour game)
Werner Kruger [4]
Dean Greyling [3]
Gerhard Mostert [2]
Marcell Coetzee [30]
Juandré Kruger [17]
Eben Etzebeth [85]
(11 Tests as captain)

Jacques Potgieter [3]
Pat Cilliers [6]
JJ Engelbrecht [12]
Craig Burden*
**Burden was selected as a Springbok for the away leg of the 2012 Rugby Championship in New Zealand. He and four other players were released to their provinces to play in the Currie Cup. He was never again selected for the Springboks.*
Jano Vermaak [3]
Johan Goosen [13]
Duane Vermeulen [54]
(2 Tests as captain)
Frans Malherbe [38]
Jaco Taute [3]
Arno Botha [2]
Lionel Mapoe [14]
Raymond Rhule [7]
Franco van der Merwe [1]
JC Janse van Rensburg*
**Janse van Rensburg was called up to replace an injured CJ van der Linde before the Test match against England at Twickenham on 24 November 2012. However, he was not chosen for the final 23.*
Willie le Roux [61]
Jan Serfontein [35]
Trevor Nyakane [42]
Siya Kolisi [50]
(19 Tests as captain)
Piet van Zyl [3]
Lourens Adriaanse [6]
Pieter-Steph du Toit [55]
(1 Test as captain)
Cornel Hendricks [12]
Lood de Jager [45]
Handré Pollard [48]
Marcel van der Merwe [7]
Oupa Mohojé [19]
Stephan Lewies [1]
Marnitz Boshoff [1]
Damian de Allende [47]
Warren Whiteley [23]
(2 Tests as captain)
Cobus Reinach [14]
Nizaam Carr [5]
Julian Redelinghuys [8]
Jesse Kriel [46]
Vincent Koch [21]
Rudy Paige [13]
Faf de Klerk [30]
Ruan Combrinck [7]
Franco Mostert [39]
Steven Kitshoff [47]
Jaco Kriel [11]
Bongi Mbonambi [36]
Malcolm Marx [33]
Francois Venter [7]
Uzair Cassiem [8]
Jamba Ulengo [1]
Rohan Janse van Rensburg [1]
Jean-Luc du Preez [13]
Ross Cronjé [10]
Courtnall Skosan [12]
Andries Coetzee [13]
Dillyn Leyds [10]
Ruan Dreyer [4]
Curwin Bosch [2]
Wilco Louw [13]
Dan du Preez [4]
Warrick Gelant [9]

Louis Schreuder [1]
Lukhanyo Am [15]
Ox Nché [1]
Jason Jenkins [1]
Kwagga Smith [6]
Ivan van Zyl [6]
Makazole Mapimpi [14]
André Esterhuizen [8]
Travis Ismaiel [1]
Sukumbuzu Notshe [6]
Thomas du Toit [12]
Akker van der Merwe [3]
Marvin Orie [3]
Robert du Preez [1]
Embrose Papier [7]
RG Snyman [23]
Aphiwe Dyantyi [13]
S'bu Nkosi [11]
Marco van Staden [3]
Damian Willemse [6]
Cheslin Kolbe [14]
Reinhardt Elstadt [2]
Herschel Jantjies [10]
Lizo Gqoboka [2]
Scarra Ntubeni [1]

Siya Kolisi – Bok captain

Annelee, there are so many things I can say.

You are the person who made sure there was not even the slightest thing that we had to worry about as players, our families, our friends or anyone. If we needed flights, passports, visas … no matter how late it was, you always made a plan and we knew it would be sorted out.

If our kids needed to be looked after, you were there. If my wife needed anything, you made sure it happened. You looked after my dad when he came to my first game on Father's Day and on my birthday weekend. Just seeing my dad so happy ... I will never forget that day.

You gave me my first-ever birthday cake when I was with the Springboks. I will never forget that moment. You cared so much.

You are an amazing human being, through and through. We had a connection, with both of us being from the Eastern Cape, and we got along from the first time we met and worked together. Annelee, you always put us first and you always protected us.

You have been such a huge role model, having done it for so many years. To be the first woman to do it in such a male-dominated sport, I salute you for everything you have done. I will be forever grateful.

I know so many young women look up to you and would love to achieve what you have achieved. I hope that when people talk about women in sport, especially a male-dominated sport, they will be singing your name over and over again.

I am excited to hear and read your story, and what we can learn from your journey. You are a special person, a true hero and a legend to me.

FOR THE RECORD

Annelee Murray was the 2019 Hollard South African Sport Industry Personality of the Year.

Siya Kolisi, the 2019 World Cup-winning Springbok captain, was named the 2020 Sport Industry Personality of the Year and Annelee, as the previous recipient, presented Siya with his award.

The Hollard Sport Industry awards recognise the best behind the business of sport in South Africa, which spans marketing, PR, digital, sponsorship, advertising, community investment and social media.

Percy Montgomery – Bok centurion

I had two experiences of Annelee and she would say the same thing of me. I was there for Annelee's first year with the Bokke in 2001 and then I went to Wales before Jake picked me again in 2004. In those three years, I grew immensely as a person and they were the making of my last 52 Tests.

Annelee's impact in her first year with the team was immediate and she did things that hadn't been done before. She showed a care that hadn't been there before and she was always making things better for us players and making them right. But when I played again in 2004 I could see the growth in Annelee as a person and in her role within the Springboks.

She was more settled and more confident, but what hadn't changed was just how good she was at her job. She always wanted to make every player's life easier on tour and to stop the noise around us and let us get on with playing rugby. She was a pillar of strength and will always be very special to me for everything she did for me, both as a player and as a colleague on the management team from 2009 to 2011.

Apart from organising and preparing the players before a Test match, she was just as valuable to us off the field, especially for me. She continuously gave me sound advice and support and nothing was ever too much to ask of her. She listened and I don't think anyone in the squad drank more coffee than Annelee because there was always a player wanting advice and guidance from her over a coffee. When we needed to talk, our person was Annelee.

Every man needs a strong woman behind him and she was that for me in a professional capacity and exactly what I and the team needed.

Annelee, you made my 100th Test at Newlands so memorable but your strength was that you treated every Test I played in as if it was mine and every other player's 100th Test. You cared so much for us as players and for the Springboks and I will forever be grateful and thankful.

Bryan Habana – Bok centurion

Where do you even begin to write something about someone as special as Annelee Murray, when there's so much to write about?

The memories, the friendship, the good times and the bad times, the tears of joy and sadness. So many unforgettable times and special memories.

One of my fondest memories of Annelee was on my first tour with the Springboks back in 2004 when I was an uncapped, wet-behind-the-ears newbie in the squad.

A few players went to dinner with the legendary Ernie Els and, in trying to impress everybody with my newfound confidence of being a Bok tourist, I ordered a round of drinks.

Unfortunately, I had not realised that the €100 I had with me for the evening was not going to cover the round as well as my meal!

I felt extremely embarrassed and sheepish, and didn't know where to turn, but Annelee quickly recognised my awkward situation and, instead of making a scene, quietly sorted that bill out without alerting anyone's attention or letting me wallow in embarrassment.

It not only showed me her empathy but also her willingness to always step up or step in when needed.

Tendai Mtawarira – Bok centurion

Annelee was an integral part of the Springbok team for many years and I was fortunate that my Test career coincided with the last decade or so of her term.

She was the heartbeat of the team and a mother figure to the Springbok players and their families. Like a mother, she was nurturing and caring and sometimes a hard taskmaster when the need arose, especially to the players (LOL!).

Annelee, you set the tone in terms of professionalism, especially when it came to doing commercial activities for the players. You looked out for us and made sure that we were treated well when we did our appearances under the Springbok banner.

One of the many memories I have of Annelee was when we were at a shoot for one of the Springbok sponsors, which happened to have a very demanding producer who deliberately intended to prolong the whole shoot for no reason. Annelee stood up to him and told him he would only have the players for a specified amount of time and if he didn't abide by that, we would walk off set.

This was one of the big reasons why I loved Annelee so much, she was always on the players' side and made sure we were protected and not exploited.

She was also a shoulder to lean on during hard times. In 2017, when things were getting so tough in the Bok environment with all the losses, I remember chatting to her for advice. She gave me a boost in confidence and belief, which wasn't easy at that point in time.

I dubbed her 'the fixer' because one could always count on Annelee to make a plan, from hustling for breakfast vouchers for families at the World Cup to booking visa appointments and getting seats on flights for players' families.

Her love for the players' families is what made the whole Springbok experience worthwhile. On every game day, whether in South Africa or overseas, she would make sure the families were well taken care of, from getting picked up at the airport to getting rooms at the team hotel. This put the players at ease and allowed us to just focus on playing well for the Springboks.

My wife and kids always speak about Annelee and remember her for her beautiful smile and ever-accommodating nature.

Thank you, AL, for all the special memories and for going above and beyond the call of duty.

I will certainly miss you and the Springbok environment.